THIRTY YEARS A
WATCHTOWER SLAVE

THIRTY YEARS A WATCHTOWER SLAVE
The Confessions of a Converted Jehovah's Witness

by
W. J. Schnell

ABRIDGED EDITION

A Division of Baker Book House Co
Grand Rapids, Michigan 49516

© 1956, 1971 by Baker Book House
Copyright renewed by Mrs. William J. Schnell
Reprinted in 2001

Published by Baker Books
a division of Baker Book House Company
P.O. Box 6287, Grand Rapids, MI 49516-6287

Printed in the United States of America

Library of Congress Cataloging-in-Publication Data is on file at the Library of Congress, Washington, D.C.

ISBN 0-8010-6384-1

Scripture is taken from the King James Version of the Bible.

For current information about all releases from Baker Book House, visit our web site:
http://www.bakerbooks.com

CONTENTS

FOREWORD

By the Lord's grace I am a Christian. I was found by God
in my tender youth. Early in life I was inveigled to join
the Watchtower Organization, and subsequently became
totally enslaved to it. As my spiritual life ebbed, I tried desperately to come free. Each attempt only resulted in deeper
slavery. Twice I thought I had come free, only to backslide
into its pit. But now, again, I am free.

By the Lord's grace I came free when He lifted me up
from a night of prayer, and when I became so agitated and
alive once again spiritually that I made a vow unto the
Lord. That night I came free!

In writing this story of my thirty years of slavery I am
fulfilling this vow, which by the Lord's grace brought me
freedom. It is not a learned treatise you are going to read
here. It is simply the heartfelt story of a slavery so deep,
that it took me thirty years to get free. In revealing how
such slavery is accomplished, I am serving a Christian purpose. If you are already engulfed in this slavery as one of
Jehovah's Witnesses, I know these revelations will help
you evaluate your situation properly, and instead of grop-
ing in the dark, you will grasp at your only way out, which
I had to learn after much searching of heart and after many
tries and errors. If you are not one of Jehovah's Witnesses,
then by reading this story of my slavery for thirty years,

you will be forewarned and will be on the lookout. In any case, this book will present to you a great boon. The ink used to print may bring to view the words that make up this story, but its spiritual concept and ideas were written with my life blood and with my feelings of torment and torture experienced in a Hell far more vivid to me than was the Inferno of Dante.

I have no rancor against my former brethren—I have no axe to grind—in writing this story. I have only one major task to perform, and that is

I have a vow to fulfill,
   which I made to God,
      when He set me free,
         once again to be a Christian!

W. J. Schnell

✛ one ✛

IT APPEARED
SO HARMLESS

■**Called of the Father**

I was called by the Father when I was twelve years old.
On a Sunday morning in July 1917, while attending a Sunday school class in the local Lutheran Church I was deeply
stirred by a vision of Jesus, our Saviour, as evoked by a
description of the parable of the Good Samaritan. Our
teacher's description of what lay behind Christ's telling of
the parable raised in my heart a keen desire to learn everything I could about Jesus. I saw that His concept of help-
fulness transcended nationality, religion and class. I sensed
that His broadmindedness in doing good was in strong contrast to what was going on around me as World War I was
dragging into its third year. All this fired my imagination
and became a challenge in my mind, to be resolved only
by learning everything I could about Jesus and His teachings, as well as about His background.

Upon returning home that Sunday noon I began actually to devour the four Gospels, then the whole New Testament and finally the whole Old Testament. I became

deeply involved in what I was reading. In later years I realized what happened here was that the Father had called me, in the manner that Jesus had promised, "No one cometh to Me, except the Father call him" (John 6:44). For through this avid study of Scripture I came to the realization of my great need for a Saviour, and a deep yearning took hold of my heart and filled my mind. I was enabled to see my situation as a human, brought into this world under the sentence of sin and death, and feelingly and meaningfully I could cry out with the psalmist, "Behold, I was brought forth in iniquity; and in sin did my mother conceive me" (Ps. 51:5).

With this growing knowledge of my true condition and a comprehension of God's provisions for my salvation in Jesus, who is not only the Good Samaritan but also the Good Shepherd, there came into my heart faith to believe in these wonderful provisions of God for me in Jesus Christ. I began to believe in sin and salvation. I learned with joy that for sinners like me Jesus had died on the cross, and that His blood had washed away my sins, and that in His resurrection death has been conquered for me and for all who accept Him in faith.

■ Raised to Fall

I am of a generation of men who as children lived in Europe during the first World War and who had all stability and peace of mind destroyed for them long before they matured. Many of my contemporaries sank in the abyss of despair; others became atheists; still others became fanatics and militant Revisionists, revolting against the status quo. To have been raised to newness of life at so young an age and under such conditions was a great boon to me. I know now that it sustained me throughout the years which followed. It was given to me by the Father through

Christ Jesus, entirely undeserved, wholly of grace—something I have never forgotten.

In my fourteenth year I was constrained by the spirit to turn myself over to Christ Jesus and through Him to the Father as dead unto my flesh and former life. I had actually become alive in the Spirit and thus came into relationship as son with the Father, into a "newness of life." Needless to say, so powerful were the inner wellsprings which were unleashed in my innermost being, that my feet jumped for joy, and my heart sang happily, and I saw everything in a new light. My whole viewpoint toward the world in which I lived was changed, and all desire for its pleasures and wealth faded from my eyes and mind, as I entered into what a certain Christian poet so eloquently calls "my Christian Spring."

In those troublous times, many of my generation became pawns used by forces which eventually led them either into Communism, Atheism or Nazism. I eventually fell victim to an even greater ISM and became its loyal slave for about thirty years of my life, namely, THE WATCHTOWER RELIGION. Astutely, as I will show conclusively in my story, the Watchtower Society utilized the unsettled times and conditions of that uneasy period from 1919 to 1938, in order to fashion a New World Society, which they hope will last a thousand years.

■ Stranded by War

I was born in Jersey City, New Jersey, in the year of 1905, and at the age of nine was taken by my parents on a trip to their homeland, Germany. This trip was undertaken in the early spring of 1914, the month of May to be exact, when war seemed very remote. When it finally became clear that war would break out, my parents tried desperately to get passage to the U.S.A., but in vain.

My father, not as yet being a citizen of the U.S.A. but having his first papers, soon was drafted in the armed forces of the Central Powers, having been a reserve officer before emigrating to America. He had to leave my mother, myself and a brother, sister and another sister to be born in September, behind. We acquired four acres of land and a house in the eastern province of Posen in Germany, situated only about sixteen kilometers from the Russian border.

War had broken out only a fortnight before, but already the Russians were swarming all around us in the woods, infiltrating the entire border area. Then, suddenly, our whole region became an armed camp. Soldiers were quartered in all our homes and bivouacked in the fields around us. The Germans were preparing for a grand offensive, the hub of which was being driven home on the fields of Tannenberg in East Prussia, where von Hindenburg annihilated vast Russian Armies. The rumble of cannon could be heard in the distance. Then one morning began a three-day march of tens of thousands of Russians, who had been taken prisoner, through our village, which was situated on a main highway in the East. Thereafter the battlefield advanced deep into Russia.

During all that time we had not heard from our father. Finally, in early 1915 we did get word from him. But in the great strategic retreat of the Austro-German Armies in early 1916, the Division in which my father served was assigned to hold the Russians back in a rear-guard action below Pzemischl. There they held the entire Russian Army for seventy-two hours allowing the main forces to retreat behind the Carpathian Mountains. Needless to say, the Division was completely decimated. The Company my father was in was reduced to only seven effectives, and these ragged remnants found their way through the mountain passes into Hungary. Again during all this time we had no word from our father and our hearts were heavy. It was specifically in this period of time that I became receptive to the message of Jesus Christ in the parable of the Good Samaritan.

My father was allowed to stay in Hungary to recuperate for six months. In the meanwhile the Austro-German counteroffensive succeeded and drove the Russians out of Galicia and deep into Wolynia far into the Ukraine, liberating Galicia. Congress Poland and other eastern areas, which were largely denuded of inhabitants, had to furnish much-needed food supplies for the Army. Teams of officers were formed in Hungary and were given charge of thousands of Russian prisoners who were to farm these vast areas. My father belonged to such a team of three officers, which was given charge of a large estate on the River San, below Lemberg.

During this time my father had a wonderful opportunity to practice Christianity. He helped wherever he could and dealt squarely and friendly with these poor Mushicks of the Russian steppes, whereas his fellow officers were harsh and cruel. This situation obtained until the Fall of 1918, when the Austro-German Armies collapsed in the East and found themselves trapped in the midst of Slavish people who bitterly hated the Germans.

The Russian prisoners broke loose and first killed off all the German officers they could lay their hands on. Remembering the good things my father had done for them, the Russian prisoners captured my father and whisked him away in the dark of the night, put him upon a fleet horse, and guided him through all the confusion and breakdown of order in Eastern Galicia, from Lemberg to Pzemischl. There my father was able to board a freight train which brought him safely into Krakow three weeks later, a trip which normally took twelve hours by freight train. From there he was able to get a train for Breslau, where he was eventually mustered out.

Late in December 1918, close to Christmas, father walked into our home. What a joy! But it was only short-lived. Early in January 1919, Polish insurgent forces jumped the gun and began occupying the Province of Posen in which we lived and which had been ceded to them by the Armistice. Once again our village became a battleground. One time my brother and I, caught in a house between a school in which were stationed German troops and our home, had to spend considerable time in a potato cellar while machine guns barked overhead. Finally the German forces capitulated and such citizens as my father were interned as hostages. For a while the future looked dark, since many of the internees who were for-mer officers and officials were being shot.

One night a bandit group carried out a raid for food in our village. They took all our food from us and lined up the women, among whom was my mother, as hostages. It looked for a while as if the leader was going to have all the women shot. I crept up close to my mother who, as I could see, kept up her usual courage. I had a German dag-ger concealed under my sleeve; for I had resolved that at the moment he gave command to shoot, I would plunge the dagger into his back. But thanks to the Lord, that con-tingency did not arise! The command was not given and the women were eventually released.

In early 1921 we were herded into cattle cars and shipped across Poland to the new German frontier and there turned over to the Germans. Three German officials took us in hand and shipped us to a refugee camp in the western section of Berlin. The day we arrived in Berlin, the *Spartakists,* a nickname for the Commies in those days, were fighting pitched battles in the streets with Republi-can troops. Everything was topsy-turvy; but at long last we were comparatively safe.

▪ I Become Involved

Grateful to the Lord that we were all alive and that we could once again live together in peace, my father and I resolved that henceforth we would spend all of our lives serving God in one way or another. Lost in this huge city of Berlin, we were one day visited by a Bible Student who left with us some books which we began to read. Not long thereafter, we looked up the Bible Students and began to associate with them. We had no other affiliations, and in the Berlin Bible Student Ecclesia we found a goodly measure of brotherly love and happiness in fellowshipping. I was then about sixteen years old and began to grow in spiritual matters.

Let me say here that these Bible Student *Ecclesias* then were a far cry from the present meeting places of Jehovah's Witnesses known as Kingdom Halls. Entirely independent from a central control, they selected their own Elders from the spiritually mature within their midst, in accordance with Paul's instructions to Titus and Timothy. We observed that these people were consecrated Christians. They were rugged individualists, greatly concerned with making their "calling and election sure," and in being transformed into the likeness of the Lord in their thinking, their living and their behavior, as well as their works in their daily lives.

When they gathered in their meetings on Sunday for a Bible discourse and Wednesday night for a prayer and experience meeting, they came to be edified, and to contribute toward such edification themselves. The meetings were true feasts of fellowshipping and Christian love. They were highly instructive—never authoritarian and arbitrary as are now the meetings held in Kingdom Halls of Jehovah's Witnesses. Those who came to these meetings were not only concerned with each other's spiritual welfare, but arrangements were made for visits to the sick and the needy, and funds were provided by the Ecclesia to lend help when needed. These meetings were filling a void in the life of my father and myself. They were a spiritual blessing to us.

Works of charity occupied a considerable time of the Bible Student groups. Not only did they help the needy of the congregation but often outsiders, wherever such were found. We would bring such unfortunates in and feed and clothe them. After we had taken care of their physical needs, we would minister to them more valuable things of the Spirit. Many were in this way salvaged from despair and brought into the communion of Christianity.

▪ I Become Active

The Bible Students spent much time telling other people about their faith, about God's purposes, and about the salvation to be had in Jesus Christ. Of course, growing up in such an environment I soon began to practice preaching of this sort. Between 1921 and 1924 I was able to continue my schooling, getting some academic education. Every afternoon I would spend two hours, from 3 to 5 P.M., going from house to house to tell people about God's purpose. I felt, as did those of my brethren, that the prevailing uncertainty among the people everywhere called for special measures, special preaching efforts, in order to bring them nigh to real hope and salvation. That was the original motive of the practice of going from house to house.

By the Lord's grace, though very young, I became highly successful. On one occasion, which even now stands out in my mind after all these years, I met with a lady who said she was possessed of demons. (There was much of that during that period of time in Germany.) She began to tell me of her plight and of the tortures to which she was being subjected. Seated as I was, looking at this lady whose face was a white pallor, and whose hair was combed close to her head with eyes deep in their sockets, I became so scared I was unable to rise from my chair. Finally, when I realized she wanted me to say something, since I could not rise from the chair I simply sank from it upon my knees and she followed suit. For a full half-hour I prayed, instinctively pouring out the woman's trouble before the Lord and asking the Lord to help her. When we finally arose from our knees she asked me to come back. Later, after many visits, she became a Bible Student. Still later she told me that her trouble began disappearing while we were in prayer during that remarkable half-hour on our knees. Being completely at a loss how to cope with such a situation, being only a mere child of seventeen, I threw myself upon the Lord and put myself into His hands; and He did not let either of us down. That experience was a token of the mighty strength and power which God is willing to pour into man for His service. I will never forget what I learned that day! Had I not gone out and brought the good news of salvation as every Christian should, trying to help people in distress, I would certainly have been the loser.

During these three years, while going to school and working in Berlin as a school boy, I was used of God to help seventeen people become Christians, three of whom had been atheists, one an anarchist, one a Communist. (Berlin was full of these godless groups right after the war.)

This was all done, as was the entire preaching work of the Berlin Ecclesia in those years, by inner impulsion, not by organization compulsion as now practiced by the Theocratic minded Jehovah's Witnesses. It was done in Spirit. Paul says in Romans 10:10, "For with the heart man believeth unto righteousness; and with the mouth confession is made unto salvation." This truth was demonstrated by these Berlin Christians. I had so very much to be thankful for, and I realized that I must do with all my

God-given might what my hands found to do, and what my zeal made me capable of doing. Many others felt the same way.

There were, of course, many who did not feel that way. However, such were not importuned to go and preach if they did not want to do so. They were allowed to fellowship with us, and we continued to help them to see more of God's purposes. I noticed that eventually many, of their own accord, would step in when the occasion presented itself to them and would acquit themselves as men in Christ. When that happened, great was our rejoicing; for it was evident that this had been wrought by the Lord, and not by use of psychological force of a Society or some Company Servant.

In November 1921, since I had not yet been water baptized, I gladly fulfilled that Scriptural injunction and requirement. It appeared to me that spiritual things began to come easier and clearer to my ken from that day on. It seemed as if the heavens were opening up to my consecrated mind and heart. It pays to be obedient to all things commanded by Jesus Christ, and I soon realized that I had become a bona fide "new creation."

Let no one misinterpret this chapter as an evaluation or approval of the doctrinal tenets of the Bible Students. I am only trying to explain what it was that drew me to them. This is necessary to describe how and why I became involved in and finally enslaved to one of the world's most dictatorial and autocratic systems.

✤ two ✤

EARLY
MACHINATIONS

■Trouble Ahead

While all this was going on, and while we rejoiced, dark clouds were gathering on our spiritual horizons! Into the background of the tranquil scene lurched the new leadership of the Watchtower Society far away in Brooklyn, N.Y. The leaders were feverishly reorganizing their work, endeavoring to recapture their former position amidst the brethren everywhere and their standing with the Bible Student Ecclesias, which they had enjoyed under the leadership of Charles T. Russell. The ambitious new President, Judge Rutherford, was an astute student of human nature, and his wrath at having been put in jail for alleged un-Americanism knew no bounds. He had to have his revenge against the clergy whom he accused of having put him there. Recognizing the potentialities of the unstable conditions throughout the world, he aimed to use them to build the second tier of the Watchtower edifice, upon the first layer built by Charles T. Russell.

The Watchtower leadership sensed that within Christendom were millions of professing Christians who were not well-grounded in "the truths once delivered to the saints," and who would be rather easily pried loose from the churches and led into a new and revitalized Watchtower Organization. The Society calculated, and that rightly, that this would yield vast masses of men and women, if the whole matter were wisely attacked.

In this way there came to be formulated a plan for a grand and persistent attack against organized Christendom. Religion was smeared as being the cause of all evil, and the fact that it was organized was proclaimed to be the cause of its wickedness.

▪Brainwashing

This new attack was spearheaded by a pamphlet entitled *The Fall of Babylon the Great* (1919) which purported to tear to shreds the basic arguments for the organized structure of Christendom. Because of her use of the principles of organization, the pamphlet boldly proclaimed Christendom to be the "Babylon the Great" of Revelation. The first phase of this brainwashing was to destroy old concepts, and ideas connected with them, which were loosely held in the minds of millions of church affiliated Christians—which task in those years, as it still is today, was a very easy matter.

But, of course, attacking and detonating Christendom as Babylon the Great was not enough in this brain washing process. When you tear something down you must put something in its place. That is the true secret of successful brainwashing!

What was this positive replacement of ideas to be? In Christian circles it is and always has been an evident and accepted fact that Jesus has earned eternal life for all those who believe. This Christian doctrine, "that those who believe on me, shall never die" (John 11:26), as spoken by Jesus, and which is as old as is Christianity, the Watchtower Society suddenly purported to have discovered as a brand new truth, or "new light" which it had gotten from the secret place. With Machiavellian cunning they culled it out of the body of Christian doctrine and put this pearl into an artificial setting of words of human interpretation. They then presented it as a new Watchtower doctrine, with the catch phrase: "Millions now living shall never die," and expounded it in a booklet bearing that title (1920).

Coming at the end of a period when millions had died on the battlefields and in the hospitals, and at a time when multitudes had suffered because of shortages of food, amidst turmoil and strife, this was an electrifying statement! By twisting this marvelous statement of hope made by the Lord, they made it appear that now for the first time could this fact be realized by this generation, and then only if men would leave Christendom behind and join the Watchtower Organization. Note how the twist to this ancient Christian doctrine was administered. While Jesus said in John 11:25, "I am the resurrection and the life: he that believeth in me, though he die, yet shall he live; and whosoever liveth and believeth in me, *shall never die,*" the Watchtower Society was saying in effect, "He that liveth and believeth in the Watchtower Organization and joins us and carries our books, booklets and magazines, and reports time to us, and attends our meetings to the exclusion of all others, shall never die." They knew that they were safe, since thousands would never see through this inconsistency.

Thus the brainwashing process began in the initial phase by the indoctrination of new and old converts to the Watchtower way of thinking, setting up the Organization's views as the Scriptural ones; and continued by gradually instilling intolerance and narrow-mindedness in the body of adherents. To be sure at this stage the Society's goal was still far from reality; but as my story unfolds you will marvel how cleverly and persistently this goal was pursued until Theocratic thinking, blind loyalty, and goose-step mass action was demanded of every adherent.

In Berlin, we were as yet blissfully ignorant of the purport of these two worldwide moves: *Fall of Babylon the Great* and *Millions Now Living Shall Never Die.* We might have known, since the slogan was concocted by the Watchtower Society and did not fit into a Scriptural setting at all. But we blindly put out millions of copies of both. I put out as many as a thousand copies of the pamphlet *Babylon the Great* in Berlin during the course of a single week and sold thousands of copies of *Millions Now Living Shall Never Die.* I would spend all day Saturday travelling on the *Ring-Bahn,* a railroad which runs around the outer periphery of Berlin, standing in the third class compartments witnessing loudly about *Millions Now Living Shall Never Die,* and selling the booklet for 25 pfennigs. Some Saturdays, huckster-like, I would dispose of three hundred copies getting about 75 Reichsmark contributions for the Watchtower, all of which I would turn over to their representative. Thus many of us, including myself, helped forge about ourselves a straight jacket which later made many of us slaves of the *Theocracy.*

■ "With Feigned Words Making Merchandise"

No one can read the history and literature of the Watchtower Society without thinking of Peter's words: "Through covetousness shall they with feigned words make merchandise of you" (2 Peter 2:3). Time and again they cited words of Scripture, tore them out of their setting, and misapplied them to suit their own purpose. And they did this with the eventual goal of selling books to obtain contributions of money to build up a worldwide Watchtower Organization. This strategy proved so successful that it has been constantly used to this day.

From the beginning this trick was used to get the people to buy and read Watchtower published books and booklets. These writings always contained a kernel of truth, particularly at the beginning, as bait. But the whole was so weighted down and intertwined with organizational jargon as to set the befuddled reader's head in a whirl. Before the unwary victim realized it, he had surrendered all individualism, abandoned all personal thinking, and given up all private initiative.

All this was designed to put the one who listened to these words into a position where he would read only the Society's books, booklets, and magazines. After he had acquired a taste for that kind of fare, the one so brainwashed was not only led into believing this Watchtower literature, but in his new position as "Kingdom Publisher" he was compelled to peddle this literature from door-to-door as the truth of the Gospel. He observed Watchtower set and inspired hours and worked submissively to attain a book placement quota. He could be compelled against his wishes and inclinations to go into certain territories, place certain books, and report the time spent in doing so.

Can you think of a clearer example of men being made merchandise through the use of feigned words?

Here is a striking example of how the Society pounced upon Scripture which might serve its purpose. Everywhere there was unrest and uncertainty following World War I. What better passage of Scripture could they find for their purpose than Matthew 24? This passage, so they contended, referred definitely and specifically to the times at hand. Of course, in making this claim they conveniently overlooked that the rumors of war and nation rising against nation, as it occurred in 1914, was not unique to that age; it had occurred before.

Besides, our Lord in the prophecy of Matthew 24 was speaking of something quite different. He was answering questions of His disciples, put in this way: "And Jesus went out from the temple, and was going on his way; and his disciples came to him to show him the buildings of the temple. But he answered unto them, See ye not all these things? verily I say unto you, There shall not be left here one stone upon another, that shall not be thrown down." Our Lord noted how His disciples were still tied to the buildings, the temple and city of Jerusalem, and how much they thought of these things. All of this, He prophesied, would come to an end amidst horrible conditions of tribulation, such as the world had never before seen. The question concerned a specific situation, and Jesus' answer applied to that particular situation. Nowhere is there here evidence that this passage has reference to a time in which one specific World War would release a chain reaction such as the Watchtower read into the events which followed the War of 1914–18.

Why then should the Society use this passage? Well, it served their purpose. By misusing this Scripture and tying it in with the prevalent unrest following World War I, the Watchtower Society created a psychological backdrop to give apparent deep meaning to its advertising campaign. All this was brought to a climax with the statement of the 14th verse, "And this Gospel of the Kingdom shall be preached in all the world and then the end shall come." This gave prophetic color and completely justified its book-selling campaign!

The clever superimposition of prophecy over the world background following the war was a masterstroke if there ever was one. It followed a pattern which the Watchtower Society has used ever since with great cunning, consummate skill and great financial and organizational success! This is the pivot upon which revolves the entire strategy of its world-wide proselytizing campaign.

∎"Advertise, Advertise, Advertise the King and the Kingdom"

In order to build a worldwide organization, the kind of Watchtower Society which Judge Rutherford envisaged, much money was needed. Somewhere between 1919 and 1922 the leaders, in typical American business fashion, hit upon the idea of promulgating a vast worldwide advertising campaign to sell books and booklets published and printed by the Watchtower Society, and from their sale to raise the money required to build the anticipated huge world organization. For a kickoff they used the Cedar Point Convention in September 1922.

But here they faced a problem. If they were to advertise the Watchtower Society, such a move would get them nowhere. The Watchtower Society was in disfavor in America, and by Presidential order had been dissolved, and its officials, from the President down had been arrested and convicted. Certainly you could not advertise that, unless you used it exclusively with the Germans. But what then would they advertise? Their books? No. But they were not stumped. They had learned well the advantage of coming with feigned words in order to make merchandise of the Word of God—and of those who would be inveigled to carry such a message.

They decided to tie their advertising campaign to the age-old Christian hope of the Kingdom of God and to give additional weight by using the parting command of Jesus to His disciples, "Go ye therefore, and make disciples of all nations, baptizing them in the name of the Father, and the Son, and the Holy Spirit: teaching them to observe all things whatsoever I commanded them; and lo, I am with you always, even unto the end of the world" (Matt. 28:19, 20). Did they not there have every necessary warrant for their bookselling campaign? In ostensibly using this mandate, they gave their campaign the forward focus of the time of the end, and gave the impression that they were now commissioned in a special way over and above the age-old commission. So those in attendance at the Cedar Point Convention saw printed upon a huge scroll as it slowly and dramatically unfolded from the top of the stage down to the platform during the Convention at Cedar Point, the striking slogan: "Advertise, Advertise, Advertise the King and the Kingdom."

Christians know that this advertising campaign of Christ and His kingdom began back there in A.D. 33, and has been carried out without interruption by the followers of Christ all over the world throughout the last two thousand years. But the truth of the matter is that it has always been done inadequately and never on the scale and with the zeal and enthusiasm which wholehearted devotion to God demands. By using the slogan of "Advertise, Advertise, Advertise the King and the Kingdom," Watchtower leaders cleverly hoped to set up an electrifying contrast, and thus unobtrusively to cover the true purpose of their campaign—to sell Watchtower published and printed books, booklets and magazines in order to raise money, to build the sinews for world organization and to spread their kind of thinking!

From that time on Watchtower leaders continued to utilize a historical background of Scripture to establish the legality of their campaign, and its correctness. They used Israel's experiences as a budding nation from her Exodus to the building of Solomon's temple as a blueprint for the buildup of their Organization. Inferentially they used the Exodus Scripture, especially Exodus 11:2, 3: "Speak now in the ears of the people, and let them ask every man of his neighbor, and every woman of her neighbor, jewels of silver, and jewels of gold. And Jehovah gave the people favor in the sight of the Egyptians." This the Watchtower Society used to buttress their thinking to give the color of legality to their going out and despoiling people of the world, whom they glibly called "Egyptians," in order to build up their Organization. Later I will show how profitable this campaign became for the Organization.

✢ three ✢

ENTERING
WATCHTOWER
SLAVERY

■Individuality Submerged

From 1925 on, the Bible Students were confronted with a real problem which resulted from the newly emerged Watchtower policy. The issue was really this: Shall we continue to develop our Christian individuality and buy out our time between birth and death as a new creation; or shall we give in to the Watchtower concept, buy out our time between birth and death by selling books and collecting money therefore and turning it over to the Watchtower along with a report of our time spent in this work every month? As time wore on, those placing the largest number of books, spending the most hours each month in the selling campaign and turning over the most money, were the favored ones; and those who continued buying out or redeeming their time in bringing forth fruits of the Spirit, were increasingly belittled, and were gradually pushed out, and finally marked as "evil servants."

In various Ecclesias of Bible Students there was only a slow recognition of the meaning of these trends. Believing in their hearts that every man must decide such matters for himself, as guided in his study of Scripture by the Holy Spirit, such groups failed to sense the danger facing them in the dynamics of the situation as provoked and sustained continuously from Brooklyn, by the Watchtower Society.

■Entering Slavery

During these times the Society was also undergoing a far-reaching organization process. Offices and printeries were expanded, and the mechanics of the big advertising campaign were being developed. Orders for books and booklets and pamphlets were beginning to pour in. In Germany at that time it became necessary to move the Society's offices from Barmen in the West to Magdeburg, in central Germany, where large properties were purchased with American dollars from monies already received through the bookselling campaign in America.

It was during that time that the Director of the German Branch began recruiting help in Bethel at Magdeburg. On August 18, 1924, I entered Bethel, headquarters of the German Branch of the Watchtower Society. Little did I realize at that time that I was entering into slavery so profound that I would not be able to emerge free again as a Christian until thirty years had elapsed, and I had spent the greater part of my life. Little did I realize that I was leaving Christian individuality behind and was entering into a sort of Zombi existence, half individual and half mass. I then and there became a cog in the machinery of one of the greatest subversions of all time.

Like most Bible Students in those days I had always been largely concerned with making sure of my calling and election as a person, and with fellowshipping with my brethren in Berlin or in our local Ecclesias. I was but vaguely aware of and only loosely concerned with the doings at the headquarters of the Watchtower Society in Brooklyn, or in Magdeburg for that matter. Like most Bible Students, I still took for granted the Society's status as set by itself when it was still young and humble, namely that it was "the beast of burden" for the brethren. As such it provided us with helps, Bibles, and with the magazine the *Watchtower,* which it published. We saw no reason why an organization should not do such chores for us.

■ A Marked Contrast

As soon as I entered the Watchtower Service at Magdeburg I felt a chilling change.

In Berlin I had moved in the circles of one of the largest Ecclesias of Bible Students in the world and had thoroughly enjoyed it. The spirit was one of brotherly love and freedom. Ours was an association of Christians, who were spirit-begotten, and who through Christ had a personal standing before the throne of God. All this was for the purpose of fellowshipping and edification.

From out of such fellowship and association I entered into the brisk organizational atmosphere of the headquarters of the Watchtower Society in Magdeburg. In the place of fellowshipping came emphasis on charts, and quotas, discussion of production policy, figuring of cost, and concern for organization. Instead of guidance of the Spirit we heard the directing voice of the Watchtower leadership. Personal freedom was replaced by blind loyalty to the Watchtower directives. While in our Bible Student meetings in Berlin we had occasion to have the "Holy Spirit testify with our spirit that we are children of God," we now had to listen to the Company servant testify that we were good Kingdom Publishers in measure that we had fulfilled the quotas set for us.

The greatest contrast lay in the fact that while our Ecclesias had been an association of Christians, the meetings I now attended in Magdeburg consisted of a "mixed multitude." By no means all were born of the Spirit. And that pattern has been followed in the Kingdom Halls to this day. At one time, early in 1931, there were the following Watchtower governed classes in association: Mordecai-Naomi class, Ruth-Esther class, Jonadabs, "people of goodwill." As will be explained later, Jehovah's Witnesses of the Jonadab class are told and themselves assent that they cannot ever be spirit-begotten but get their fructification through association with the Watchtower Organization.

While this condition prevails throughout Germany today, there was only one place where such was the case in 1924. And I had to go there, and that voluntarily!

▪ Serving at Magdeburg

Though I was only nineteen years of age I readily fitted into the Magdeburg picture. The novelty of the situation appealed to me. Having been reared among Germans I was an obedient boy, trained from my earliest days to respect the instructions and commands of my elders and superiors. I also carried within me the native love the Germans have for orderliness and organization.

I wound up in the office and was soon engulfed in the promotional work of the magazine *Das Goldene Zeitalter (The Golden Age)*. I became instrumental in bringing about copy distribution rather than subscription distribution, or a company carried out distribution on a local level. The result was that from 1925 to 1927 we saw the edition sky-rocket from 50,000 copies to 325,000 copies per issue.

It appeared that I was here in my element, and more and more I was led into and became deeply engrossed in organizational schemes. I lost sight of "my first love." As I became thus involved I found less and less time for self-contemplation, for study of the Bible, and personal religion. I spent very little time living and "walking in the Spirit" and more and more time catering to the Watchtower Society and its tasks. Needless to say, my "new creation" life dwindled to a mere flicker, and in place of living in "newness of life," I began again the life of the old "beggerly elements." The dream of a "World Society" (which then I could not yet visualize as a slave society), like the dream of a new and great Germany held by millions of Germans of my generation, had replaced the reality of a life in Jesus Christ.

■ Predictions of the End of the World

The Watchtower Society always has been marked by a degree of eccentricity. They loved sensationally to predict dates for the end of the world. They had originally predicted the end of the world for 1914. But in that year many Bible Students who believed this prediction were left in the lurch when the Kingdom for which they looked failed to appear. This, of course, left a bad taste in the mouth of many. It did not, however, dismay the leaders.

During the ensuing years, especially in the pamphlet *The Fall of Babylon the Great* and in the booklet *Millions Now Living Shall Never Die*, the Watchtower Society merely switched to 1925. They kept that new date prominently before us and all the people, as the year when the Kingdom would come with the reappearance on earth of the Old Testament worthies or the princes amid Bible Students.

This expectation was fanned by every publication of the Organization of that time and it left a deep imprint upon our minds. In fact, it virtually made irrational crackpots out of many of us. For example, I well remember that in the fall of 1924 my father offered to buy me a much needed suit of clothes. I asked him not to do it since it was only a few months to 1925, and with it would come the Kingdom. This now seems utterly ridiculous to me. Even if the Kingdom as expected had come, I meanwhile very badly needed new clothes.

The Watchtower Society kept fanning this great expectation to a high pitch. It used this expectation to create a background of hope, and focused it on a date they hoped to be ready to expand their advertising campaign of the Watchtower Kingdom.

However, at that time some of the more mature among the Bible Students began to catch on and to notice the discrepancy in the Society's statements about 1925 being the beginning of the Kingdom and the end of the present wicked world, and the Society's increasing activities of buying land, buildings, ordering printing presses, all making for expansion! The two just did not go together.

∎ A New Nation—Conceived in the Watchtower

With the advent of 1925 came the unmasking of the true plan for a world organization as envisaged by the Watchtower Society. Early in that year came also the laying of a doctrinal change. In the *Watchtower* article, "Birth of a Nation," the Watchtower Society began to build up its organizational idea. Rightly it pointed out that Christianity was to be "a nation of kings and priests." But, after having stated this glorious Scriptural truth, the Society went about to subvert this concept by proclaiming itself to be that nation; or rather collectively those organized by them to be this new nation.

While Peter conclusively showed that each Christian as an individual would be a part of that nation under God and Christ, the Watchtower distorted this concept and interpreted it to refer to a class. Thus this new nation, born in 1925 through the effulgence of the *Watchtower* magazine, was to have as its end composition: a Faithful and Wise Servant Class, a *Theocracy* of gold, ruling from the top down, as well as a *Theocratic mass* of unspiritual Jonadabs, who have no part in this Kingdom or Nation, but are absolutely subject to its bidding. Such subjects would not only be enslaved by this new nation to think as did the ruling class, but also to work exactly as commanded. This concept, as we shall see, embedded in the article "Birth of a Nation," has been minutely carried out.

Thus during this artificially created period of great expectation, when there was a hopeful looking forward to the Kingdom and the appearance of the Princes, there emerged a new *Nation* within the nations of the world which eventually in a universal sense would become a new world society. This new Nation thus was conceived in treachery, dedicated to the principle that all men are not equal but must be divided into classes, and organized for the proposition that all subject to it are Theocratic slaves. And it envisaged a slave society to last for a thousand years. Far-fetched, you say! Watch how it will be proved in this book by incontrovertible facts.

■ "Covenant or Sacrifice: Which?"

In 1925 appeared still another *Watchtower* article which was revolutionary. It was titled "Covenant or Sacrifice: Which?" Graphically it put the concept of character or individuality into juxtaposition to a new concept, namely that of a Kingdom Publisher.

Individuality had hitherto characterized all Bible Students, typifies all bona fide Christians today, and has marked all who ever were truly spiritbegotten. The child of God has through Jesus Christ entered into a highly personal relationship with God, the Father. So highly personal is this relationship, and so important its aspect, that such a new creation can only grow and mature as it receives the Holy Spirit sent from the Father. In this walk in the Spirit, the individual Christian progresses in the light of the Gospel toward that day when in glory he will be one of the priests of that Nation of kings and priests. Naturally, under such activation, the watching of one's personal conduct, and the improvement of one's life by synchronizing it with the concepts of Christianity, are of paramount importance. In Bible Student circles that was called "character development."

The Watchtower Society, bent upon utilizing all the time of its prospective slaves to advance its advertising campaign, now came out with the premise that this character development was a sacrifice of individuality, and that it kept such Christians from fulfilling their part in the Covenant. Claiming to be the mouthpiece of this Covenant, the Society pointed out that in thus catering to himself and his individual standing with the Lord, a person was foolishly squandering his time and not redeeming it.

Furthermore, so argued the *Watchtower,* a person was like a die or a character. No amount of development or cultivation could change him who had been so moulded or cast. It would therefore be wiser for the Bible Student to leave individual application of Christianity behind and to strike out and operate on a wider plane.

From this argumentation it followed that such persons would do better if they became Kingdom Publishers. The time they now foolishly and uselessly used for edification and character development they might better devote to preaching and selling books, booklets and magazines, attending special meetings for further training as a Publisher, and by counting and reporting all time spent in this work on report slips to the Watchtower Society. What was here proposed then was to supplant living unto the Lord with living for the Society. It was proposed that instead of bringing forth to God one's own Christian fruits of the Spirit, one would do better by bearing *kingdom fruits*. Instead of bringing praise to God in the form of works of gratitude, report slips should be forwarded to the Watchtower Society reporting all time spent in this work and carefully indicating the number of books, booklets and magazines sold. Thus the Watchtower Society actually took God's place in relationship of the Publisher.

In this later innovation, did the Watchtower Society tip its hand. Interested in the making of a huge sales campaign of 1922, they wanted to have a semblance of Scriptural backing for organizational gimmicks and records on hand. And eventually they wanted to focus the thinking of every Kingdom Publisher hypnotically upon an organization line. This was to constitute the second phase of brainwashing, namely, the annihilation of individuality into robot-like mass action, or as it is now called "Theocratic action."

These were the doctrinal and organizational switches which were evident in the early part of 1925 and which were to set the trend for the emergence of the Watchtower Theocracy of 1938. Thus was laid the foundation for the enslavement of all who would come under duress of the "Theocracy." And I was one of them!

✦ four ✦

A LOOK AT THE ORGANIZATION IN AMERICA

In order that you may understand what I had stepped into, let me review for you what had happened and was happening to the Bible Student movement in America and throughout the world.

■The Judge Takes Over

No sooner had Charles T. Russell died (1916) than there came into play a behind-the-scene tug of war for his mantle. Russell's will left instructions for certain men to succeed him. However, the legal counsel, Judge Rutherford, was able to maneuver proxies of the Corporation in such a way that he emerged President of the Watchtower Society. In order to quiet somewhat the furor which had arisen over the high-handed way in which this subversion was accomplished, he succeeded early in the war to create an issue outside of the Organization through his editorial policy of the *Watchtower* magazine, the outcome of which was to put him into the position of a hero.

As a result of the seemingly antiwar editorial policy adopted for the *Watchtower* magazine, Judge Rutherford and the other directors of the Society were arrested, the Watchtower Society was legally dissolved, and the Judge and others were tried and convicted. They were sentenced to serve an aggregate total of eighty years in the Federal Penitentiary at Atlanta, Georgia. Of course, once America won the war, Rutherford caused his friends to circularize a petition for a retrial, and eventually he was not only freed, but completely exonerated. Lawyer Rutherford had cleverly used a fortuitous situation to create a condition in which he could lessen the pressure building up on the inside of the Organization caused by his unusual election as President. He was entirely successful in taking the onus off the way in which he became President of the Watchtower Society, and utilized the arrest and subsequent conviction to create around his actions an aura of being God's servant and the chosen one to lead this "New Nation" to better things. This aura never left him to the day of his death.

The Judge in his pronouncement of 1919 had accomplished another result favorable to the Society. By seemingly opposing Christendom's support of the war, he had been successful in separating the Watchtower Society from all other organizations which lay claim to being Christian. Now it became necessary to build the Watchtower Society into a powerful organization, which would not only supply Bible Students with literature and Bible helps and arrange conventions for them, but which would focus world attention on this esoteric Watchtower, in exactly the sense as the first Watchtower of Babel was elevated over the rank and file of mankind. You will recall, that the first Watchtower of Babel was built in defiance of God in order to lead men to safety from any possible flood which might again inundate the low places. The Watchtower Society of Brooklyn was now beginning to claim that its edifice would become *the refuge* which would carry millions across the rubicon, so to speak, that is across Armageddon into the Millennium, in which it would emerge as "The New World Society" to last a thousand years.

■The Judge Plans Changes

In order to build this New World Society it became necessary to change the Organization's policy. The Organization had to be given a forward focus, with a goal and an ideal embedded in a Scriptural setting. For the time being, using as a base the books of Charles T. Russell, which were accepted everywhere in Bible Student Circles, he settled on a theme of "The Kingdom," using the World War and ensuing climactic conditions as the window dressing for the need of a worldwide witnessing campaign. His first feelers in this direction in 1919 had been highly successful. This prompted him to bring about a Convention to be held in September of 1922 at Cedar Point, Ohio, where, as previously related, the assembled delegates of the Convention were prevailed upon to pass enthusiastically a resolution sponsored by him, titled "Advertise, Advertise, Advertise, the King and the Kingdom!"

The Judge knew that it would take more than a motto to put his plans across. Up to that time the Bible Students had been of such rugged individuality types that they claimed they had fled various organizations in order to become and remain free and unencumbered in their quest of Bible studies and living as Christians. Their motto of "Non-Conformity" became a byword in the '80s and '90s of the last century. In order to sell such people the idea of a super organization required not only a policy change, but an unusual acumen. The Judge had it!

How was it done? Again by raising an issue outside of the core of Bible Students and outside of the orbit of their thinking. Taking advantage of the Bible Students' ostensible opposition to organized Christendom Judge Rutherford succeeded in becoming known worldwide as "uncompromising foe of organized Christendom." At the very time he drew this red herring across the horizon of the congregations of Bible Students throughout the world, he began to lay the ground for an organization far more absolute and far more rigidly organized than was the Catholic Church, which it so bitterly opposes. This organization not only presumes to take the place of the organized Christian Churches which were so vociferously accused and condemned by the Watchtower Society from 1919 on, but they daub their organization as "God's Organization," the churches and all others being the Devil's organization.

■The Society Puts Its House in Order

With this new coterie of men now well established in Brooklyn, N.Y., in the driver's seat as the Watchtower Society, and with this forward focused policy goal now adopted, it became necessary for the Watchtower Society to put its own house in order. It was necessary to weed out the recalcitrant elements and to close ranks, even if that meant a decimation of those connected with the erstwhile Bible Student movement.

It was evident that the hardest core of opposition to the Society's policy was to be found in the independent congregations of the Bible Students which were completely autonomous, electing their own elders, having their own preaching arrangements. The Society's books, booklets and magazines were not used as the curriculum of such meetings, but alone the Word of God formed a material for discussion and study. How to break such a bulwark of individuality and make it yield to an integrated central Organization—that was the problem.

The initial steps, as we saw, had already been taken in this direction by the Bible Students themselves with the acceptance of the leadership of the Watchtower Society as their champion so evident in the dissolution of the Society in 1918, and then later when they gave broad backing to the Watchtower Society sponsored resolution and authorizing them to conduct a worldwide witnessing campaign. Be it noted though, that only a small percentage of Bible Students accepted this policy with the majority passively acquiescing.

The next step was taken by the Watchtower Society with the publishing of an entirely new set of books and booklets, with a new slant, paving the way for total organization. This literature was intended to affect change of thinking on all such matters amidst the Bible Student congregations and gradually to supplant individual thinking with organization mindedness. In order to make such media available cheaply and in large quantities, the Watchtower Society purchased its own printing plants, and with the book *The Harp of God* (1922) began its publishing and printing career. Soon it was able to put out larger books for only 35 cents a book, coming down eventually to as low as 25 cents a book; and a flood of these began to flow out into the world.

The use of Watchtower Society published books, booklets and magazines had a three-fold purpose: (1) to effect mass thinking within the orbit of the Organization on all matters pertaining to the Scriptures; (2) to occupy all Bible Students, if possible, with the selling of these books to all mankind, and in doing so to raise issues for cleavage; (3) to form a financial backlog of funds to support a sustained worldwide increase campaign to come.

Of course, at first, only very few Bible Students would make use of these books in the congregations; and soon disagreement flared over many things expressed therein, and dissension increased.

In order to crystallize matters to the point of a crisis, the Society instituted early in 1925 a rigid method of accounting and reporting to it all time spent in witnessing with its books. Needless to say, this caused a cleavage all over the world, with many refusing to report time and placement and still others refusing even to place the Society's books. In the decade from 1921 to 1931 almost three-fourths of the Bible Students originally associated with the Society in a loose fashion left the Society. That is precisely what the new Watchtower Society had hoped to accomplish.

As a result of this decimation the Society soon had the quorum to operate without opposition among those left behind. Now they were free to ignore individuality. Without opposition they could now establish set minimum monthly time requirements for each Publisher as well as quotas of minimum numbers of books to be sold per month. Prior to that the Society depended for its operating capital entirely upon voluntary contributions sent in by Bible Students. But with the worldwide bookselling program now in full swing, money soon came pouring in, making it possible not only for them to have sufficient operating capital but allowing them rapidly to expand their plants and to move into new fields of operation. This continued even through the heart of the great "depression."

Thus the Society established a mode of "worship" within the new Organization based on business quotas and quantums, making "merchandise of men," as the Jews had done in their temple in the days of Jesus (John 2:16). The recruits for such Publishers were found in the newly orientated masses, among those trained to the idea of class thinking in opposition to individual thinking. These, of course, were in the majority after the bloodletting of three-fourths of the Bible Students had been so adroitly accomplished.

As the twenties rolled on there came a marked change over the original Bible Students who remained with the Watchtower Society. They were no longer too much interested in what they had previously termed the Christian walk in the Spirit as New Creation "making sure their calling and election." They now were openly and admittedly more interested in converting the world to their way of thinking, and to getting ever greater numbers on their side in order to set them up for "Kingdom Service" measured in terms of time quotas, book placement quotas and attendance quotas, etc. The attainment of quotas they made paramount in their thinking.

✦ five ✦

A LOOK AHEAD

In order that you may understand what I will relate concerning my experiences in Germany and later in America, it will be necessary to look ahead. This will furnish valuable background, without which much what I have to say would be meaningless.

■ Class upon Class

The Watchtower Society was bent on eliminating the last vestige of individual thought and action within her ranks. The result was the growth and ripening of classes of new converts in the places of individuals as before. They were thus ready for the next step, that of promulgating and officially designating classes within the Organization.

When the stage had been properly set, the Society began to re-create itself into a super class. Thus they established themselves as "The Faithful and Wise Servant Class" "to whom all goods were given," in order to eradicate once and for all the old Bible Student belief that Charles T. Russell had been that "faithful and wise servant."

It is interesting to consider in retrospect the procedure which the Society leaders used to create the classes. A multitude of followers was spawned from their large seed beds through mass distribution of Watchtower books, and was watered by means of book and Watchtower studies in the budding Kingdom Halls. This mass of followers was sedulously trained to become entirely dependent for spiritual food upon the issuance of a bimonthly issue of the *Watchtower,* and to expect yearly some new Organizational truth in a book and some lesser truths in booklets, new enough each time to tickle the ears of the classes who itched for fabulous things. As this process gained momentum there came doctrinally and actually into view as a natural and almost necessary development, first the Mordecai-Naomi class, next the Ruth-Esther class, and finally the vast Jonadab class. Note that each class emerged on a lower strata, and the lower the strata the larger the numbers, denoting the weakening of quality of the new converts, reminiscent of the Theocratic image structure in Daniel 2:31–34, with its head of gold, silver breasts, brass loins, feet of clay and iron.

Those of the Mordecai-Naomi class had been told that they were the last members of the organized Christ on earth. This "Christ" consisted of Christ Himself and 144,000 members. When many of this first class became unfaithful in not catering to the Watchtower Society, the Mordecai-Naomi class was replaced by a younger class of recruits, the Ruth-Esther class. It was conveniently discovered that the door to the heavenly calling had not been entirely closed on the heels of the Mordecai-Naomi class. There was just time for the Ruth-Esther class to come in. In fact, the door to the heavenly calling, according to Watchtower light, was actually in the process of closing as they were entering. But with their entry the door was closed and Christ was complete. They next proceeded to create a larger class, but one much lower, over which they would serve as a protective umbrella and upon whom they could work from the top down. This new class known as Jonadabs, was referred to as "the hewers of wood and the carriers of water," using as a pattern the slave relationship of the Gibeonites to Joshua and the Israelites (Josh. 10:10–27). The Jonadabs are not regarded as brethren in Christ; for the Jonadabs, so it is claimed, cannot be spiritbegotten. Remember, the door is shut! Thus, since most Jehovah's Witnesses today are of the Jonadab class, it follows that the majority of the Jehovah's Witnesses no longer are Christians.

There you have the three classes, and raised up to cover them all, to teach them all, and to feed them all, is the Watchtower Society as "The Faithful and Wise Servant Class."

From that *fatal* day on members of these classes have believed every fable that the *Watchtower* editorial committee has invented and devised for their "edification," even though this committee has time and again had to reverse itself. From all this it is evident that these classes have blindly allowed to be raised over themselves this class of teachers, whose doctrines they follow solely because it tickles their ears, and whom they allow to entitle themselves "The Faithful and Wise Servant Class" with headquarters at 124 Columbia Heights, Brooklyn, New York.

■ To Everyone a Penny

The Watchtower Society now, as "The Faithful and Wise Servant Class," began its world advance. A preparatory move was to declare these Watchtower sponsored classes to be the component parts of "The New Nation." Thus they used the old trick of creating the doctrine of extra-territoriality. This presumably put all of their practices safely outside the pale of criticism. With this the Organization was ready to be thrown into high gear.

By now, tens of thousands were coming in as products of a brand-new Watchtower gospel appearing in newly published books, booklets and magazines, written solely to appeal to the itching ears of such new converts. But soon more and more of these so-called "converts" felt that they were not meant for heaven. This sort of thinking, of course, was encouraged by the Watchtower Society; for, having committed themselves earlier to a Christ organized of 144,000 members only, they had unwittingly limited the expansion of their Organization. This had to be corrected. So the Society conveniently declared its own position to be that of the Remnant of Christ on earth, or the last ones; and the position of all now coming in to be of that of "the Great Multitude," who no longer could be such a spiritbegotten class.

In order to create Scriptural backing for the switch from a limited class of servants of Christ, to the vast populations of Watchtower slaves, which they wanted to take into the Organization, the Society used the parable of the Penny (Matt. 20:1–16). They interpreted the Watchtower Society to be in the parlance of this parable "the vineyard of God," and the twelve years from 1919 to 1931 to be the twelve hours of the parable. They declared that this work day had now come to a close and that the Watchtower Society as "the Faithful and Wise Steward" to whom all these goods had been given was now about to pay out the Penny. At the convention of Columbus, Ohio, held in 1931, at the end of that Watchtower described day, the Watchtower Society gave their new converts, and the ones still with them, a new name, "Jehovah's Witnesses." That new name was their Penny!

The reward for both the Remnant or Christians, and the Great Multitude or un-Christian Jonadabs was the same. This was the lever used to indicate the amalgamation of both types, as symbolized in the image of Daniel 2:31–34 by the mixture of iron and clay in the legs. Thus these "witnesses," a vast mixed multitude, were indicated to be the "leg men" of the Organization.

Those who might murmur against all alike receiving this same name, "Jehovah's Witnesses," would be like those in the parable who had come early into the vineyard and who had murmured upon seeing the latecomers get the same reward. In this manner the Society leaders now claimed themselves alone to be "The Faithful and Wise Servant Class," and as such alone qualified to reflect new light and dispense truths from the temple, which they claimed they received direct from the face of the Lord.

Thus by 1931 the Watchtower Society had eliminated God's word by substituting for it their own books as the new seed; and replacing it with the Society's books, booklets and magazines as the containers of "food in due season." It had replaced the only name under heaven by which we might be saved, Jesus, with that of its own Organization; and had effectively terminated the tenure of Holy Spirit as the fructifier of God's word in the minds and hearts of Christians, and put themselves, as a Theocracy, in that place.

Finally in order to streamline their Organization the Society officially promulgated in 1938 "The Theocracy," and had every company of Jehovah's Witnesses, by resolution, vote away their autonomy in spiritual matters. In this the Jehovah's Witnesses agreed to accept without question the Society's teachings, and to bow abjectly to her supervision. They further granted the Society the sole right to come into the congregation and to appoint servants from Brooklyn to be their Theocratic Exactors—Zoneservants, who in turn would be "the eyes and ears" of the Society. This second wave of brainwashing thus resulted in the complete subjection of individuality into Theocratic Mindedness, which arrangement they now fully termed "God's Organization."

In the meanwhile they had also broadened the basis of the Organization by establishing branches and organizing the work in one hundred forty countries throughout the world. They had also built Gilead Watchtower College in which to train hundreds of missionaries of the Watchtower Kingdom, to be sent out into the world as emissaries of the Society.

Thus, the Watchtower Society has become a world Organization, changing in a mere thirty years from independent congregations of Bible Students to a "Theocracy" already talking in terms of World rule, as the coming "New World Society." Thus the classes: Mordecai-Naomi class, Ruth-Esther class and Jonadabs or Great Multitude without spiritbegetting, are now all commonly embraced under the name Jehovah's Witnesses. They have over them the Faithful and Wise Servant class, or the Watchtower Society. So Jehovah's Witnesses today bow and abjectly worship the gods of Brooklyn, which they have raised with their own hands into a high Theocracy.

Yesterday lowly placed individuals; today a class THEOCRACY; tomorrow A NEW WORLD SOCIETY!

✧ SIX ✧

THE JUDGE VISITS GERMANY

■ Early Days at Magdeburg

The Bethel of the Watchtower Society, or its German branch, was situated in Magdeburg, Germany. It had just recently been moved there from Barmen in the West in order to facilitate better and more efficient organization. Of course, everything at this time was topsy-turvy in the Magdeburg office.

I was assigned sleeping quarters in the attic of the Crystal Palace, which was the name this well-known building had before it was bought with American Watchtower dollars. There was no staircase as yet, and we had to climb to our sleeping quarters by use of a ladder. Some of the brethren jokingly said that by means of this ladder they were ascending and descending the Watchtower Hell, in contrast to Jacob's ladder. Those who had said that soon left the place altogether, as you can well imagine!

In the cellar of this Crystal Palace we were actually printing early in 1925, a million copies of the book *The Harp of God* in German, working around the clock, seven days a week. This was war—*a campaign*—and demanded an all-out war effort.

My first job in Bethel was to sit on a stool in front of a revolving disk-shaped platform which in separate compartments contained the various sections out of which the large *Harp* was fashioned. It was my job to pick up the several sections in sequence, placing them on top of one another until I had a complete book in my hand. It then went to the bookbindery, where it was sewed, glued, covered and pressed. As yet we did everything rather crudely, but we put out an enormous number of fine books.

■Instead of the Princes, the Judge

By the spring of 1925, when the world was supposed to come to an end according to the expectations raised by the Watchtower predictions, and the princes were scheduled to appear to us, there appeared in their place Judge Rutherford. He came with a pocket full of American dollars, which the Society had collected in the form of contributions for books, and soon bought us a brand new plot of land, and buildings, and machines. As soon as he left there began a year-long expansion program.

An amusing incident took place at the time of the Judge's visit. The Director of our German branch, as had many before him, had grown a large beard, patterned after Charles T. Russell's beard. The Judge did not want anything at all to remain which might remind him of Russell—not even the cultivation of a beard. So, sitting at the table for dinner one night within my earshot, the Director asked the Judge for one more large rotary press. The Judge said nothing for a while, merely ate. Then suddenly he looked up, his eyes pinned severely on the Director's huge beard and said, "I will buy you the press if you take that thing off," pointing to the beard. It surely shocked the

Director's sensibilities, but he meekly heeded the warning and soon shamefacedly appeared minus his beard.

■ The Magdeburg Convention

Judge Rutherford's visit was synchronized with a large Convention in Magdeburg, which lasted three days. The registered number of conventioneers was about 12,000. Actually 15,000 appeared! Since there were no facilities to take care of so large a crowd in the provincial town of Magdeburg, we had to improvise. We rented large circus tents, and set them up in a field outside of Magdeburg. In this field we installed temporary plumbing. We organized a cafeteria, wherein we served hot meals for a nominal price. This was the first cafeteria ever organized in Watchtower circles, and so successful was it as a moneymaker that the Society has long since adopted it as a regular feature for its conventions and circuit assemblies throughout the world. Shelter for this vast throng was obtained by signing up rooms with householders who were previously solicited by careful canvass. This, by the way, was also a first, and is now used everywhere in conjunction with Watchtower Conventions and circuit assemblies.

I was in charge of the pre-Convention transportation arrangements. I was told by our now beardless German Director to try to make as much money as possible to defray expenses, so that we might show the Judge a good financial report. We organized fourteen special trains from all parts of Germany and devised a little celluloid tag container, with room to insert a white card with the name of the congregation typed into it. These cost us about three pfennigs apiece and I sold them for fifty pfennigs. We made a nice piece of money from this transaction to augment the Society's coffers!

This Convention was the scene of a master execution of a switch.

On the eve of the Convention, while having dinner with the Judge presiding over the assembled Bethel family one hundred fifty strong, we were addressed by the Judge. In eloquent manner he pictured himself in the Atlanta prison pacing up and down in his cell. "Then," said he, "I gripped the iron bars of my cell, and looked up to Heaven, and promised the Lord: 'If thou wilt get me out of here, I will never cease to expose Christendom, and I will cause this Gospel of the Kingdom to be preached.'"

Against the background of this vow he told us of the new vista ahead. Assuming the role of seer atop the high Watchtower of the Society, his eyes took on a faraway look and he began to tell us that we should not selfishly anticipate going to heaven now in 1925, when there was so much work still to be done on earth. He was letting us down! Our pent-up emotions tied in with our expectation for the end of the world were being deflated. But, in doing so he took us high up on the Watchtower with him, as high as the mountain of temptation which overlooked all the kingdoms of the world, and he showed us a great world organization! He pictured vast billions coming out of all the kingdoms of the world, person after person and class after class, slowly learning the Kingdom. He envisaged mountainous stacks of books to be published and printed.

So paternal in its attitude toward the Bible Students had the Watchtower Society become, that as a climax the Judge condescendingly used one of Jesus' miracles as a mass token of benevolence. He magnanimously fed each one in the multitude of 15,000 at the last session with one hot dog on a bun and some potato salad! The impression that he was a great benefactor emphasized by this last act of the Convention, was so well engraved that for years afterwards in my travels throughout Germany all of the many things that happened at that momentous Convention—

loss of individuality, loss of congregational autonomy, loss of freedom, enforced time reporting, etc.—most attendants remembered the one free hot dog and potato salad! Clever Judge!

■The Judge's Blueprint

What the Judge outlined at the Magdeburg Convention clearly showed us that he was operating along lines of a well-laid master plan. The plan had been taken from the experiences of Israel from the day they were liberated from Egypt (and he underscored that with the name he gave the book just then published, namely *Deliverance*, 1926) through their wilderness journey and to their entry into the land of promise and finally to the establishment of the Monarchy, and reaching its superb climax in the building of the Temple of Solomon. It was not until July 1938 when, in discussing the advent of the Theocracy of 1938, the Judge again used the expansion and building program conducted by Solomon as his Scriptural base, that the pattern fell in place in my mind. I was then catapulted back to this memorable dinner meeting on the eve of the Magdeburg Convention in 1925. Reference to the building program of Solomon formed his closing remarks then, too. Thus, throughout all these years, from 1919 to 1938, the Watchtower Society had used the experiences of the formation of the nation of Israel as a pattern for the formation of the New Nation, improvising freely wherever and whenever it suited its purpose, intent upon improving vastly over Israel.

In following this pattern they even included the loss of individuality within Israel as they chose the monarchial form of government. Also the final effect of such a program upon the Monarchy itself, when it broke in two after Solomon's death, was not forgotten. For eventually they used this to justify a third and more exalted tier for the Watchtower Society, where it would be controlled no longer by one man, as had been the first by Russell and the second by Rutherford, but now by a perpetual *consortium* at the top, or by collective leadership. This third layer was inaugurated in 1938. They were not going to repeat Solomon's mistake!

Much of the Judge's talk had little meaning for the Bethel family that evening, because the translator was not very skillful. But I, being American born, understood and absorbed every word.

∎ I Did Have Moments of Misgivings

What I heard and saw soon caused me much searching of heart, and much turmoil of mind. With much misgiving of heart I often lay awake at night wondering what had happened to my ideals as a Christian "new creation." I worried about all this hustle and bustle, and the constant changes taking place which were riveting stronger and stronger chains around my person. I was becoming Organization-minded to an alarming degree. And then there were those things that did not fit together. For example, on New Year's Eve, in 1925, we celebrated with prayer the advent of 1925 at Bethel, hoping for the appearance of the princes and the Kingdom that year. But at the same time we were expanding the material possessions of Organization!

By the spring of 1925 the Society sent out a call throughout Germany for carpenters, bricklayers, plumbers, to build a shiny new Bethel factory and buildings. This affected a reorientation in my mind. Embued with success and advance I now became totally and zealously Organization-minded. By that time I had begun to succeed in building up the edition of *Das Goldene Zeitalter (Golden Age);* and since nothing succeeds like success, I finally became completely absorbed in this task, forgetting about myself completely and of my standing as a Christian. Prayer and studying, now carried on only in crowds, became stereotyped, and all individuality rapidly disappeared from my thinking.

As I have said, once in a while at night while alone in my bed, unable to sleep because my mind was disturbed, would misgivings rise in my heart. Then would I remember those days of my "Christian Spring," when it had been so important to me to be assured of the Lord's approval on every act of the day before falling asleep. Now I seemed only concerned over the fulfillment of production quotas and other Organization tasks. Had I, in becoming part of a worldwide organization, "gained the world and lost my soul" (Matt. 16:26)? If I had, I certainly was not profiting by it spiritually, financially or otherwise. Much later, on February 15, 1951, when, after having piled up a record of twenty-two years of full time service with the Society, I was no longer willing to perform or conform, and I was taken off the list and my entire record with the Society blotted out, was I to learn that it had not profited me to gain position as Kingdom Publisher in the worldwide Watchtower Organization and lose my soul or individuality. Thus back there, my misgivings had been quite well placed.

✤ seven ✤

SIFTING

▪ Conform—or Else

Occasionally I returned to Berlin to visit my friends, and my parents. In coming back I would only find that, as elsewhere, the policy of the Watchtower Society was creating havoc in the Berlin Congregation. Many respected Elders were forced to resign under a cloud of unfaithfulness while others were shoved into the background. I could tell every time I returned that a new and younger group was gaining ascendancy with the Society's help, while the old timers were being pushed out whenever they refused to adhere to time and book reporting, using the Society's forms.

At the same time an organizational change was being effected. Service Directors were being appointed by the Society. For a while they were merely the helpers of the presiding Elder of the congregation. But soon the Service Director gained the greater influence, as the Society addressed all mail and company matter to him rather than to the presiding Elder. This was done on the premise that the Service Director was the servant of the Society, whereas the presiding Elder was the servant of the congregation. In this manner the Service Director became established and recognized as the official representative of the Watchtower Society. By 1927 most Elders had been pushed into a corner or out of the congregation entirely, and the Service Directors had taken over completely.

Such like myself, who were young and aggressive and mechanically loyal, were usually appointed to the position of Service Director, and in performing our tasks we often carried them out ruthlessly without regard to gray hair and venerable service of the past. We were trained to lead in this hatchet work, by moving in directly and pushing or forcing our elders and betters out, without regard to Christian ethics and brotherly love.

In this manner, and to my everlasting shame, I was used in a middle German town where there was a congregation of one hundred seventy-five Bible Students who would not accept a Service Director, nor would report time or carry out Watchtower Society instructions. I was sent there from Magdeburg, a mere stripling of twenty-one years of age, with the full backing of the Watchtower Society to make that congregation toe the line, and with specific instructions to split them up if they would not come around.

Confronting me were men whose hair had grown gray in the Lord's service, fine Christian Elders; and I, a mere youth, overrode their objections preemptorily by asking the congregation after an hour's discourse, "Who is in favor of the Watchtower Society?" Upon receiving no answer I took it upon myself to brand the members of that congregation as "Evil Servants," and asked all in favor of the Watchtower Society to rise and follow me out of that hall. Eight of the one hundred seventy-five assembled followed me out and we repaired to the home of one of the brothers and there organized a new congregation. I, of course, became the Service Director.

To back me up in this arbitrary action, the Society gave me *carte blanche* (full power), allowing me to use three truckloads of Publishers brought in from Magdeburg every Sunday, although this was some one hundred kilometers distant. Soon, with such pressure behind it, this new congregation was as large as the old one had been. But what a difference in the personnel, and in the spirit of the personnel! No longer were there gentle Christian men and women in here, but purposeful, energetic book salesmen and Publishers, out to make their mark!

In similar fashion this purge was carried out ruthlessly throughout the land and finally a new concept of congregation emerged. The Service Director, who represented the Society, gradually attained first place in the congregation as the Society's instructions multiplied. Finally the Society in one stroke, through a *Watchtower* article, eliminated the position of Elder in the congregations. That was done, so they said, because election of Elders was unscriptural. Actually it was done to end control of congregations from the local level, and to usher in a top down Theocratic arrangement from the control tower in Brooklyn.

■ "Sifting" at Bethel

All this had required in the first place a reorganized Bethel office fully in harmony with new Brooklyn policy. This step was accomplished in Bethel from 1924 to 1926, to which time my discussion has now arrived. During the time of readjustment all recalcitrants were carefully weeded out. This necessitated a terrific turnover of personnel.

It was agreeable to all of us that the Watchtower Society did not pay anything for services rendered, since we felt we were serving the Lord; and being unencumbered and single we required nothing but food and shelter and a few clothes. However, in these new rules the Society was exacting what amounted to thought control as well as behavior control, after the fashion of a penal institution. Many felt that this was unwarranted. These naturally refused to sign the house rules and this new code. This achieved exactly what the Society wanted. The purpose behind this action was to ferret out all who might not be wholly committed to the new policy of the Watchtower Society.

The Watchtower feigned Scriptural backing for such "sifting," as they called it. They utilized the Biblical narrative of the deliverance of Israel under the leadership of Gideon from the yoke of the Midianites (recorded in Judges 7). As in the Scriptural event the number was finally sifted to a mere three hundred who drank water standing up, so they argued in the columns of the *Watchtower* would the Society finally be surrounded by a small zealous group to whom eventually would be given the victory.

This sifting in Bethel had by 1926 been accomplished. Now the Society felt it had the pure gold out of which it hoped eventually to fashion the head of gold of the Theocracy, illustrated in the image of Daniel 2:31–34. And now that this had also been accomplished within the precincts of Bethel, they felt they could extend the process of taking on a one hundred fifty kilometer radius idea. In this radius we were instructed to establish first insensibly and then more pronounced the new order of things, based on bookselling, time reporting, business meeting attendance for training, and finally *Watchtower* study for continuous indoctrination. By 1927 these congregations became the pattern for all Germany.

■ Society Double-Talk

The Society at this time kept harping in the columns of the *Watchtower* about the defection in "the Mordecai-Naomi class," by which they meant the old timers. This was in reality Theocratic double-talk, and a way of play-ing the younger against the older ones. They kept point-ing out, again by misuse of Scriptures, that a new class, the Ruth-Esther class, was beginning to appear. The impli-cations were completely damaging to the position of the older ones in many congregations, who thus were pub-licly labeled as non-conformists and complainers and unfaithful ones.

The fact that the Ruth-Esther class was everywhere replacing the Mordecai-Naomi class was a positive and tacit endorsement by the Watchtower Society of these newer and younger elements in every congregation; and, of course, it did not fail to have its immediate effects. As complaints increased from the quarter of the older ones, the Society felt called upon to come to the rescue of the favored, younger Ruth-Esther class. Quite soon, and with Machiavellian cunning, they would have the complain-ers branded as troublemakers, and would accuse the Elders of themselves fomenting this unrest. They then caused them to be arbitrarily set aside and pushed into a corner under a cloud of unfaithfulness. The incessant warfare thus imposed upon them was just too much for these gen-tle Christians who still lived in a personal relationship with Christ Jesus. They rejected the overbearing hegemony of the Servant class of Brooklyn and Magdeburg. The result of all this was that they just faded from the places they once adorned with Christian living.

▪Stooges for Brooklyn

We in Magdeburg were actually stooges for Brooklyn. We were the trial organization forming by our moves the pat-tern for the future assault on the congregations in the U.S.A. Every detail of how most effectively to subvert the congregations was tested and tried by us and was reported to Brooklyn and there filed away for future use in the U.S.A.

The larger congregations proved to be in the most troublous, since in these the Elders were generally well trained and strong Christians. But, the tide was against them! As more and more books were being placed carrying the new Watchtower gospel, and as many new adherents were coming in, we began to experiment with subjection by division. We did this by arbitrarily breaking up the whole congregation into from six to twelve units, all semi-autonomous to make them more palatable to the rank and file. We headed each unit with a specially appointed Service Director from the Society. At the same time a semblance of the unity of the old congregation was retained by arranging for a monthly two-day assembly of the whole congregation in some special place. This was the method used to make the congregations more readily manageable. It worked so well that the Society in Brooklyn, when they thought the time was ripe for it (around 1934–35), began using this same method in the larger cities in the U.S.A.

The inconsistency of the Watchtower Society in its arbitrary use of the Scriptures to suit their Organization purpose was once again glaringly shown in their interpretation of Matthew 24:45–52. The "faithful and wise servant" of this passage they insisted to be a *class* so as to nullify the previously held belief that it applied to Charles T. Russell; but the "evil servant" of the second portion of this very same Scripture they just as strongly insisted to refer to *individuals,* not a class. In short, while the Society collectively was the Faithful and Wise Servant Class, its opposers as individuals, were evil servants and were so branded. This established a justifiable cause for "disfellowshipping." This double standard of interpretation is in evidence throughout all the books and booklets and magazines of the Watchtower Society.

❧ eight ❧
GOD'S ORGANIZATION

■ A Discrepancy Removed

With the work of 1926 in full swing, it became increasingly clear that there was a glaring discrepancy in our sustained vociferous attack against Christendom because of its use of the principle of organization, and our own building of a highly efficient organization and our very evident use of organizational methods. With the London Convention of 1926 coming up, we were told from Brooklyn that something *big* would come up there which would settle this apparent discrepancy. Thus, once again, we of Bethel awaited with great expectancy the announcement of a new truth from Brooklyn.

With typical Watchtower expediency and about-face method came the Judge's justifying argumentation. And a rich one it was—and a bit hard to follow! It ran something like this. God has an organization and has had one from the beginning, from the time He started creating. But Satan stole a march on God by using the organization for himself. Satan as the "Mimic god" subverted organization

63

to his use. But there was a God's organization which was primeval, and which the *Watchtower* elucidated, was "God's woman." In this weird claim that God has an organization and that this organization is a Woman, the Society was not only justifying its Organization. It was likewise laying an esoteric basis for increase by works, rituals, time counting and reporting, book placements and book studies. The emerging new Publishers they claimed, were born of God's Woman just like children born naturally of a woman. According to this explanation, all churches and worldly organizations are Satan's organization; and all those who have come out from these under the guidance of God's Organization into Publisher relationship with the Watchtower Society have thus become the offspring of God. God's Organization then, was directed from Brooklyn, New York; Satan's organization was directed from London, England!

Thus was the crude basis laid in 1926 for what would be built upon as time went on, until the Theocracy of 1938 would emerge as God's sole representative on earth. All organizations outside of the Watchtower Society were Satan's organization. Jehovah's Witnesses now were the *ins;* and all others, regardless who they were, were the *outs!*

It is from this position that the subsequent behavior of Jehovah's Witnesses toward other organizations, and toward the nations in which they lived, was based. Their witnessing no longer consisted of gentle efforts to teach Christ and baptize believers, but degenerated into organized forays and attacks upon enemies; their visits to the homes of the people from house to house were no longer simple acts of preaching, but were a "spoiling of the Egyptians" (Exod. 11:2) by getting as many and as large contributions as possible; their visits to study groups became an infiltration of the homes of the other sheep to steal them away from Satan's organization. Laws requiring permits to regulate sales in communities were considered a "framing of mischief by law" against God's Organization. Arrest for violating such laws was in no way something to avoid or fear, for this was in reality a "persecution for My name's sake"—using the Lord's statement.

All sense of values was warped by this new Theocratic Organization doctrine and casuistry. Saluting or honoring the emblems of the State was "bowing down to Satan's image," and was prohibited. It was all right to bow down to the Watchtower Society of Brooklyn, because it had now become God's Organization; but anything not approved from there was from now on to be opposed.

Bearing arms or going to war was only proper now if called by God's Organization, just like it had been for the Israelites when they fought the Philistines. Jehovah's Witnesses never were opposed to war, nor are they conscientious objectors in the true sense of the word. They believe that all the wicked shall be killed; and by "the wicked" they mean all who are not of God's Organization, the Watchtower Organization. In fact, they preach that all such who are of other organizations unless they flee to the city of refuge, meaning God's Organization sponsored by the Watchtower Society, shall be destroyed. And in issues of the *Watchtower* they have asserted that in Armageddon, when all the wicked will be slain, the little children of such wicked will also be slain. Climaxing all this they conjured up the "rain of fire from heaven," the savage prognostication of a coming total mass destruction in Armageddon of all men outside of the Watchtower Organization.

In answering as to how to treat opposers to the truths promulgated by the Watchtower Society, if they were once members of the faith and have recanted, representatives of the Society often say: "It is impossible to kill them, as the laws of the land do not permit that. But were God's law in effect [meaning, 'were we as God's Organization already the New World Society'] then they would be killed.

The best thing to do under the circumstances is to treat them as if they were dead."

We were not long in putting these concepts into practice. But before I get into that, there are a few important points which I should further explain, and which occurred subsequent to the London convention.

■The Incentive Plan

The main aim of the Watchtower Society was to increase greatly the sale of their books. Each year a new book penned by Judge Rutherford made its appearance. It was necessary to spark these intermittent sales campaigns with all sorts of inducements. We of Bethel were asked to take the lead, and since we received very little money for our work, we were told we could augment our income by making special effort to sell Watchtower books. The Judge offered us in Bethel a bonus of two books free for every one book we sold. I have always been a good salesman, and though I only used Sundays for these sales forays, because I had to work weekdays in Bethel, I sometimes sold twenty-five copies of *Deliverance,* getting fifty books free. And when we were arrested we pleaded that we were preaching and not making money on that, when in this case we full well knew we were getting a 200 percent profit!

It was very disturbing to me as a Christian (and I still liked to feel that I was a Christian) to realize that my conscience was being hardened by this organizational casuistry. To this day those of Bethel and the Pioneers sell their books at a profit. Yet when they are arrested for peddling without a license they claim they are preaching, as did we; and, as I will show you later, they have made that claim stick!

The incentive system in the form of a profit-sharing caught on, and soon the Bethel reports were featured in the *Service Director,* a monthly Organization paper. This made good reading and caused many congregations to emulate us. When once this pattern was established and reports began to come in of huge sales from all parts of the country, such reporting became standardized, with totals appearing in the monthly *Service Director.* Next came the setting of national quotas, the emergence of charts, and all the paraphernalia of well-geared sales organization. Our sales began to skyrocket! In the quotas and in the reports the Society now had the levers through which to exert pressures.

If there were congregations where there were no Society boys or rooters, we had to visit them and force the issue, or as we would say, "Build a fire under them." "Place books by the millions!" was our slogan. After all, the primary purpose of the *"Advertise, Advertise, Advertise the King and the Kingdom"* campaign which began in 1922, was to sell books!

▪Kadaver Gehorsam

It was very important at that time that the buildings which were now in the process of building should be speedily completed and put to use. Our congregations, our sales outlets, were crying for books—more than we could supply.

The Society had invited volunteers from all over the country to help with the building. It was soon found, however, that since these were volunteers they worked only leisurely. It appeared to the heads in Brooklyn that the work was going too slowly, and they pressured the Director for speed. He hired three "worldly," that is "outside," gang foremen to supervise and expedite the work. These men had instructions to bear down on the brethren, to get them to work harder. This pressure was augmented by the Director from the spiritual angle. He made use of the consideration of the daily Manna text, in the discussion of which the Bethel family daily joined over their breakfast, as the platform from which to reprimand the brethren. The Director went so far as to call for *"kadaver gehorsam."* When he used those words I knew instinctively that he had gone too far. That term is a German military term, which denotes corpse-like obedience. That did it. More than half the workers quit in short order, and many others left quickly thereafter. In fact, it became a problem to get new workers to fall for the call from outside their own country.

The leaders in Brooklyn coldly marked that result down for future reference. After all, our experience in Germany was to become the blueprint for the Theocracy later to be established in America. It bothered these Watchtower leaders very little to set foreign taskmasters over their brethren, in almost the same manner as the Egyptians had done to the Israelites, whose later history they after all were using as a blueprint for the establishment of the New Nation. Much less did it bother them that such behavior was contrary to established Christian principles. What did matter to them was the fact they learned that the brethren will not take to slavery under *outsiders*. They filed that valuable information away very carefully; and when the Theocracy of 1938 was established, and thereafter, when they began to use Theocratic Exactors and taskmasters to drive on the Kingdom Publishers (or better, Kingdom *slaves*), to a better quota performance, to larger placements of books or more regular attendance at the meetings, they used *brethren!* "Servants to the brethren" they call them now. It seems that most of Jehovah's Witnesses, having sunk so low in individuality thinking and having descended to the nadir of a Zombi-like existence, will put up with slavery if it is forced upon them top down theocratically by their own taskmasters.

Needless to say, they did have to hire outsiders to complete that building program in Magdeburg!

✦ nine ✦

FROM ZEST
TO DISGUST

■New Zest for Action

The time had now come to put the new concepts of God's Organization *vs.* Satan's organization into practice. We got the go-ahead signal and went to work with usual teutonic thoroughness. Our whole attitude had now changed. We were on the inside of God's Organization. No longer, as in the old Bible Student days were we following the command of Jesus in Matthew 28:19–20 to disciple the nations for Christ, to become Christians. Oh no. That was far too tame. We were now the *ins* and all the others were the *outs* in relation to God. They had better get *in* with us as God's Organization or suffer the consequences which would automatically accrue to Satan's organization in Armageddon!

You would be surprised what the adoption of such a premise can mean to a people. Instead of having the humble attitude born of the vision of a Christian ministry, we became conquerors and warriors. Feeling that Christendom had failed, we felt that as God's Organization we held the commission to go through the midst of Christendom and mark all that sighed and cried for the abominations done her and lead them out into God's Organization.

Since Christendom was using the name of Jesus, or that of *Christ,* prominently, we felt that the time had come for us to tone down the name of Jesus and put the name of Jehovah in its place. After all, we had to be different from Christendom. But in rejecting the name of Christ we were at the same time rejecting the idea of a living Christian personal relationship with God on an intimate basis, and the concept that salvation comes through faith in the blood of Jesus Christ, and not through works set up by an organization. We became *Jehovah's* Organization; and in name and practice we were led to ignore Jesus, "the only name given under heaven whereby men can be saved." We took Jehovah's name for the vain purpose of proclaiming our organization as God's Organization.

■ We Press the Battle

We, as God's Organization, were going to conquer the earth as a land of worship. Fired by this credo we attacked, and we attacked everywhere—in halls, in mass witnessing parties in small towns on Sundays where people were attending their churches, from house to house during the week, in copy circulation of magazines and their fortnightly delivery. Again using the terminology of Scripture we pressed "the battle to the gate."

Naturally we caused strife and dissension, and finally experienced attacks on our persons and arrests in towns and villages. But we had become fanatics and were willing to pay the price cheerfully. We were sold on the fact that we were soldiers, and we were carrying on overt acts and sanguine warfare against he entrenched enemy, Christendom. Forward then, come what may!

At this time Storm Troopers of the National Socialist Party were beginning to appear here and there. They soon singled us out, proclaiming that we were American propagandists organized from the U.S.A. One of my meetings was broken up by Storm Troopers while I was speaking and I was hit over the head with a heavy oak chair. Many of us were arrested everywhere and mob action came into view here and there. The Protestant churches sued us for blasphemy of God. There ensued in the Supreme Court of Saxony a seven-day trial, which we won. The Roman Catholic Church moved in to drive us out of Catholic Bavaria and especially in the Fulda region; but we hit back in mass action.

In arresting us and in the multiplying of court cases, our opponents did us great service. It caused our ranks to close tightly, brought about genuine interest in our Organization by people dissatisfied with things in Germany, and set us up as martyrs. We naturally continued to bait the enemy to further overt acts. Because of all this publicity our books were selling like hot cakes! Our placements were by the millions, our new converts by the thousands! "God's Organization" was marching on.

■We Fish in Troubled Waters

In the Germany of the Wiemar Republic everything was going from bad to worse. Unemployment was rampant and hope for better times was fading everywhere. Communism on the left claimed millions and the Nazis on the right were growing fast. In the middle, however, were millions who wanted a spiritual and peaceful way of life, and these were the people we were after. We were fishing in the troubled waters of the German population.

Appearing to them as God's Organization, powerful, unafraid of opposition (actually bearding the lion in his den, so to speak), we easily became their champions.

If events had not transpired to put the Hitler movement into control, Germany might have become the first Jehovah's Witness state of God's Organization. The Nazis and the Communists realized this and began really to oppose us as the third force. Even though our work in Germany came to a sudden and violent end with the advent of the Nazi movement and government, we in Germany had laid for Brooklyn the pattern and the know-how. This sort of thing could be done in America when the time should be ripe.

▪We Go In for Mass Production

Our factory in Magdeburg had by this time been completed and the Watchtower Society sent to us from Brooklyn an expert on the Taylor system, to teach us this mass production system. Several of us, using stop watches, began to clock and time the movements of the personnel.

We found that some brethren tired after four hours of making certain movements—for instance, horizontal—whereas if they were put into a job where the movement was perpendicular they could keep producing all day without letup. We soon began shifting the force in accordance with aptitude. But this created a furor amidst the brethren. We made short shift of complainers, and asked them to leave as fast as they began voicing opposition. New workers came in gladly from the ever increasing reservoir of new converts who were so much more eager than the older ones, and who were much easier to train and much more amenable to instructions.

At that time too we were taught the value of cost figuring. As a result we succeeded in producing our one Reichsmark book for but 12 pfennigs, which was even better than the Brooklyn factory's cost of a 35-cent book for

4 cents. This left us huge margins of profit since our distribution costs were nil. All Publishers paid their own expenses in the field, doing their bookselling during their spare time. We did have Colporteurs and Pioneers, who got the books for 20 pfennigs and kept the 80-pfennig difference. In America the 35-cent book was given to Pioneers for 8 cents at the time.

We were not allowed to make public our financial statements, lest we get unfavorable publicity. Had we done that, our opposition would soon have caught on to the basic purpose of the worldwide witnessing campaign. In fact, whenever large capital expenditures were made— and our plants were constantly expanding—we did not use accumulated funds. Instead we borrowed from the brethren on the basis of issued bonds. This same principle was used in Brooklyn. This procedure eliminated unnecessary questions regarding our financial statements, and gave the appearance that we were a financially poor organization.

Our factory became so efficient and our leadership and organization was so successful, that Brooklyn soon put us in charge of Poland, Czechoslovakia, Romania and Austria; and we were named printers for the Scandinavian countries. It is my considered opinion that the Watchtower religion would have emerged as the top religion of Europe, if its forward march had not been stopped by World War II in 1939.

Not only did Brooklyn gain valuable data from our ascendancy in Germany from 1919 to 1932, but the war years also proved to be invaluable years for conditioning. They brought to flower The Watchtower College of Gilead at South Lansing, New York. In the world focus of this movement, this Bible School is to Jehovah's Witnesses, what Eton, Cambridge and Oxford have been to English diplomacy and statesmanship.

■ I Get into Trouble

Accustomed to speaking my mind, I soon got into trouble in Bethel. Believing in my right to express my opinions, I soon learned that if anyone wanted to get on, he had to keep his opinions to himself. I gradually learned to say very little in answer to questions at the Bethel dinner table. I just rattled off the current Organization jargon, using *Watchtower* published slogans like "great privilege," etc. I slowly began to hate myself for it, and from conversations with others I discovered that many others did too.

Then in late 1926 I was "called on the carpet" and given a good dressing-down for shielding a number of brethren who did not want to sign an arbitrary pledge in order to remain in Bethel. It was my responsibility to get all to sign, and I had failed to report the names of those having conscientious objections regarding the matter. I was able to keep that quiet for more than a year, when one of the many *Watchtower* spies, with which the Bethel family was interspersed, found out about it. The Director shouted, "I know everything you do, whether in the office, or out in the field or in the Kingdom Hall."

I learned then that while secular governments allow their citizens to claim conscientious objections to certain things, the Watchtower Society certainly did not grant this privilege to members of the Bethel family. *Kadaver gehorsam,* or corpse-like obedience, was still the policy. If amidst "God's Organization" even today you dare to voice conscientious objections to anything the Society of Brooklyn wants or teaches, you automatically become an "evil servant" and are summarily condemned. No mercy, no leniency, no respecting of a person's convictions are allowed or permitted. If it had not been for the fact that I was a good lad otherwise, being in the forefront of the work, I would have been condemned and dismissed for shielding the brethren. It was a warning I never forgot.

■Unrest in Bethel

A veritable revolution did take place inside Bethel, the center of Theocratic power in Magdeburg. With the Organization expanding, with methods being improved, and production stepped up and sales going beyond dreams, little consideration was being given to a person's likes and dislikes. We, of the rank and file, were well fed, and by now had modern living quarters far superior to those enjoyed by most of the families from which we stemmed. But our time was all rigidly organized and strictly regimented, with three meetings a week, six days (and often seven) scheduled for work. That did give rise to dissatisfaction.

There was no favoritism shown anywhere except to those who were the Director's spies and pets. They received all kinds of favors. Most of those we saw favored sooner or later turned out to be spies and stooges. Everything said and done by us was somehow reported to the Director, and he would often tell us, "I know everything as soon as you say or do it. So don't!"

A dossier section, manned by a network of spies and undercover brethren in the country congregations and in Bethel, was instituted, to record all our missteps. This dossier, or file of unfavorable evidence, was not used unless and until a member got a little out of line. Then he was with startling suddenness faced with this accumulated information. It usually shocked him, as it does any decent person, to realize that he has been spied upon. Usually he fell meekly back into line. Before the interview was concluded he would be warned that still more information was available, so as to leave a threat hanging over him like the sword of Damocles. In this way the Director was slowly but surely getting the upper hand and was making all the boys behave.

While the Director succeeded in making good Bethel servants of us, he was not much of a good servant himself. Not only was he living much better than we were, apart in his own private apartment, but he began to show it in his dress, wearing silk shirts, silk socks, and expensively tailored clothes. Remember that that was in an environment where every one of the brothers was working for 15 Reichsmark a month, hardly able to buy cotton socks and broadcloth shirts. We were often kept clothed by presents from relatives.

Besides, our Director often went on unexplained trips, sometimes disappearing for as long as a fortnight. He used first class train accommodations or traveled in style in his Mercedes driven by a chauffeur brother. This was in quite radical contrast with our methods of travel. When we were sent on Organization chores we rode third class, or five or six in a car. Our Director even used the best airplanes already back there, spending money earned by the Publishers by the sweat of their brows. Ever since then the "Messrs Big" of the Society have used the finest accommodations and most elite surroundings when on their worldwide trips.

All this finally soured so many of the brethren that the word of this dissatisfaction got to the Judge in Brooklyn. But, having some spies even there, the Director got wind of it before the Judge could take action. He immediately made reservations for an unnecessary trip to Romania, and while there behaved so badly in pressing the authorities for the release of some brethren, that he managed to get himself arrested. As soon as the Judge heard of the Director's arrest in Bucharest, he went to work to get him released. In the meantime the Judge conveniently chose to forget about the charges. In this clever manner the Director managed to save his neck. It came off later though when the work came to an end because of Nazi oppression, and our "devoted" Director turned against the Society.

■I Get Disgusted

Thus the whole Organization, while mushrooming fast, was really very unhealthy inside. It resembled the Jewish Theocracy which the Lord described in Matthew 23:27: "Woe unto you, Scribes and Pharisees, hypocrites! for you are like unto whited sepulchres, which indeed appear beautiful outward, but are within full of dead men's bones, and of all uncleanness."

Early in 1927 I had become thoroughly disgusted with things in the Organization. I could no longer endure the torture and torment in my mind prompted by such things as the suppression of Christian thinking and service in favor of Organization mindedness, and the banal repetition of Watchtower slogans. I realized that if I quit Bethel and stayed in Germany, I would never find peace, but would be haunted and persecuted until the Organization had gotten rid of any influence I might have. That is precisely what happened to me here in the U.S.A. from 1942 to 1954, as I will show. But back there I was able to forestall that by exercising my privilege to return to America. I sent in my birth certificate and other necessary papers and applied for a passport. In June, 1927, after a thirteen-year absence, I once again set foot on the good soil of America.

✤ ten ✤

"PIONEERS!
OH, PIONEERS"

■On the Outside

With my arrival in New York in June 1927, there came a lull in my affairs as far as my connections with the Watchtower Society was concerned. Never again was I to look upon the Organization with the personal intimacy I had when I entered its portals in 1924. Even though I became thoroughly involved with the Organization once again, it was to be a mechanical and detached involvement. Never again was it to be based on love or admiration for the Watchtower Society.

I conceived my first task to be that of getting my parents and my brother and sisters to this country. I sensed that things would go from bad to worse in Germany. All who preserved their individuality, and also all, like those of the Watchtower, who had their own world goal, would find the concentrated hatred of the Nazis descending upon them.

During this time of adjustment, between 1927 and 1931, I stayed very much on the outside of things as far as the Watchtower Society was concerned. However, as my father and other relatives, all staunch Watchtower adherents from Berlin, became acclimated in this country once again, they began to associate with the local and Brooklyn Congregations. I sensed a constant pressure being brought upon me to enter again into Watchtower service. My reluctance, owing to my experiences in Magdeburg, was cleverly brushed aside with the remark that things were not as dictatorial here as they had been in Germany.

■ America Lags

As far as my heart was concerned I was definitely on the *outside* of things, and I looked upon the Watchtower Society disconnectedly and objectively. I noticed that in every way it was far behind the Organization in Germany which had been totally organized and which flourished under the Society tutelage. The American printery in 1927 was far behind ours in Magdeburg in efficiency and capacity.

In the congregations too, they were here in about the same stage that we in Germany had been in early 1924. Elders still held sway in many congregations and many Bible students still refused fully to bow to the Watchtower Society. Witnessing work was largely carried on only during weekdays as yet. Sunday witnessing was beginning to take place, but only as it had been in Germany in 1924 by the newer elements or such who were naturally extroverts and liked that kind of thing for its own sake. Service Directors had about the same influence at this time in the congregations as had ours in early 1925 before the great purges. In fact, everything was much slower than it had been in Germany.

▪Why the Delay?

Being of an inquisitive mind and eager to analyze things, I set out to discover the reason for this delayed action. Knowing the Watchtower Society's purposes and goal, having lived with it as it unfolded in my three and one-half years' stay in the Magdeburg Bethel, I wanted to know why, in its own bailiwick, so to speak, the Society did not employ the same methods, especially since these had proved so successful in Germany.

Inquiries revealed, to my surprise, that things had to go slower here because of the character of the people. Americans rebelled at regimentation of any kind and would have to be led into a position by induction and by use of emotional and business tactics. Besides, Americans had not undergone such hardships in World War I as had we in Europe. They were, therefore, not in an unsettled condition of circumstances and living which proved so advantageous to the Society in Europe. There was nothing like this here, and of course, the Watchtower Society had to wait before launching an all-out attack like the one we had engineered in Germany in 1926.

The Society was determined to bide its time, to build up slowly their Organization methods from the inside out, carefully training personnel for future action. Then in 1929 came its golden opportunity! For almost four years America was in the pond of despair of the great depression. This was a godsend for the Society (and, of course, it claimed that the depression was another sign of the end of the world). This depression created a vast pool of people who were never again to feel secure in the workings of the American system. Here vast pools of troubled waters were forming, and soon it would be good fishing for the Watchtower Society! Here was a vast class of dissatisfied people, as if it were tailor-made for the Society's purpose.

▪ I Rejoin the Ranks

In order to get sufficient loyal personnel trained the Society initiated the Pioneer service, which was the successor to the Colporteur work under Charles T. Russell. It began to forge this group into a loyal primary reservoir of trained personnel for the time when the great push would come and the day when the Theocracy would dawn. The Pioneers became pampered darlings of the Judge, his spiritual shock troops of full-time servants. At every turn he showed his partiality to them. For example, he would occasionally send each of them a whole carton of books free of charge so that, as he put it, "they could buy a pair of shoes and walk well-shod on the earth." These Pioneers were used in the same fashion we in Germany had used the Bethelites and others closely allied with us.

The Watchtower ranks increased greatly in numbers when the depression hit. Many of the newcomers naturally gravitated toward the Pioneer service. Within my family, who now began to sense that things were beginning to move like they had begun to move in Germany in 1924, and who thought this was a blessing, plans were made to enter into the Pioneer service, too. Finally in 1931 my father, sister and her husband, pooled their resources and bought a Model A Ford. Father built a house trailer, one of the first ones I ever saw. The Society at this time was supplying blueprints for trailers. One day in the summer of 1931 they hitched the Ford to the trailer and began to Pioneer in a county of upstate New York.

During all this time I was under constant pressure from them to join them in this operation. Finally, early in 1933, after about two years of resisting, I consented. I bought a Ford coupe and joined the group in Clark County, Georgia, in which the city of Athens is situated.

■ Watchtower Charity

The reader will at this point kindly pardon a digression which is necessary to an understanding of Watchtower practice.

Since the Watchtower Organization is frankly out to establish a "New World Society," or a worldwide organization under the rule of the Watchtower Theocracy, it cannot afford to be a charitable organization. It has to its credit no bona fide charitable works, which it at best considers maudlin sentimentality. They usually justify this by misusing the Lord's statement, "Let the dead bury the dead" (Luke 9:60), or they denounce the organized charitable works of Christendom as hypocrisy on a par with the works of the Pharisees which the Lord condemned, and use the Lord's dictum against vain display of "good works." In thus upbraiding Christendom for its organized charities, they cleverly threw up a smokescreen to divert attention from the complete lack of charitable works by their so-called Christian Organization.

Yet, wonder of wonders, they do insist that they practice charity! How? Why, in their work of preaching, by going from house to house, by bringing people to their meetings in Kingdom Halls, and by selling their magazines! This to them is more valid than any and all the charity practiced by organized Christendom.

It does not bother them that they practice in the very way the Pharisees did, which manner Jesus plainly and strongly condemned. They certainly perform their acts of charity openly. They report to the Watchtower Society every hour they spend in doing such work, the actual number of books they place, the number of back calls they make, and the book studies they hold in people's houses. They stand on street corners "to be seen of men" with a magazine bag around their necks, selling magazines. In their Kingdom Hall meetings they erect charts, on which they publish the monthly result of their "charitable" works, and set themselves quotas to be accomplished throughout the year. They devote hourly meetings, called service meetings, to the open discussion of what they contend to be charitable works. And then they eagerly expect to be rewarded openly by appointments as Servants, or by a good standing in the congregation and with the Society.

With this digression over, I wish to point out that since the Watchtower Organization is not charitable in any true sense of the word, we Pioneers were soon taught not to look for any financial support from the Society in any measure. While they claimed authority to tell us how to work and how many hours to put in each month, they did not follow through with financial support. In this respect they conducted themselves as any sales organization. At that time we received our books for eight cents a copy and sold them for thirty-five cents. If a Pioneer over a period of time failed for any reason whatever to pay his bill, the Society stopped sending him books until he cleared up his account.

Most of us who entered the Pioneer service had little or no money. About all we had was the necessary initial equipment—a car, or a car and a trailer. To be a Pioneer then, required some real business acumen. Many started out, but only a hard core remained over the years.

■Pioneer Days

When I joined our family Pioneer group, we had two cars. I have always been a good salesman and before long I sold about thirty to thirty-five books a day. We soon found out that money was scarce in the country, especially among the farmers. This led us to develop a typical business approach. When we came to a new territory, we first visited a dealer, preferably one who had a grocery store and a gas station. We would tell him about our preaching work and tactfully explain that we accepted produce in lieu of money for our books. We would exchange a number of books for gas and groceries and some cash. Usually we found an "easy mark" rather quickly.

With such a system arranged, we picked our counties according to the produce available, and worked them during seasons when these were marketable.

For example, we arrived in Greene County, North Carolina, during the tobacco harvesting season. This, by the way, was the only time these sharecroppers had money, and in a few short weeks we sold hundreds of books. In order to help the Pioneers who would follow the next year, we recorded all the salient information on our territory assignment.

Once in a while we got stuck. Then we had to improvise. Often we had three or four crates of eggs which the dealer could not take, or perhaps some bags of pecans or cages of chickens. These I would then take to some of the larger towns and peddle them to people on Saturdays.

In Georgia, at one time we got into a county to which even the foxes had said "good night," and in which there was literally nothing to trade. Everyone was on relief. It looked like we would have to pull up stakes and go on to another county. We hated to do that, as it took considerable money to travel from one place to another, since we never worked adjoining counties. I suggested we make a two-day reconnaissance trip through the territory and check carefully before giving up. Soon I began to notice one or two old cars in almost every back yard. An idea hit me. I examined the wrecks and found most of them to contain their old batteries and often the nickel plated radiators. I returned to the county seat and made a deal with a garage man. We promised to deliver to him old batteries for thirty cents apiece and radiators for eighty cents each. With these arrangements completed we soon sold twenty-five books a day, accepting batteries for twenty-five cents and radiators for seventy-five cents, in exchange for our books at the rate of twenty-five cents a copy. You should have seen the faces of those poor Georgia farmers when we offered them one of our books for a battery and three books for a radiator! They thought we were a bit "touched in the head." They gladly accepted the books, for they said they now had plenty of time for "book larnin'." So, here again we accomplished the Society's main purpose of "piling up huge piles of books in the homes of the people for indoctrination"—and also financed ourselves.

On another occasion in Missouri, the rear axle of my car broke. Since the axle had to come from St. Louis, and I had only fifty cents in my pocket, I pledged my car for security to the garage man who had to order the axle. I set out that very day to visit the business district of the town and in eight hours of concentrated work I sold every book I had, taking in $19.40 in contributions. Thus I had the money long before my axle arrived from St. Louis and was installed.

Tragedy hit us in Caroline County, Maryland, on the Chesapeake peninsula, in September 1934. We were stationed in an old churchyard, under a huge oak tree. A hurricane blew in from the Cape and raged for two days accompanied by incessant rain. In the forenoon of the second day my nephew and I were seated on the front seat of our car reading. I was, strangely enough, reading the book of Job, when suddenly I noticed the branches of the old oak beginning to touch the car. That seemed very odd as the lowest branches were about fifteen feet from the ground. I suddenly realized that the tree was slowly falling toward the trailer in which sat my father, sister and brother-in-law! I jumped out of the car, ran to the trailer, threw the door open and yelled, "The tree is falling on the trailer. Get out." Having done that, I raced back to the car, started the motor, and got it clear just in time. The tree fell with full impact on our trailer, and smashed it completely. All our belongings were squashed under the tree.

We spent the night in the old church. There actually were bats and owls in the belfry that night, making it for us, with the wind still howling and the rain still falling, coupled with the disturbing experiences of the day, one nightmare of a night!

The next day we visited a man who owned an idle and unused gas station situated on a fine tract of pine woods. The man who owned it was in our book a rabid religionist who had asked us to leave his property when we had come to sell him books. He had absolutely no use for Jehovah's Witnesses, he said, and thus we were naturally hesitant about going to see him. To our surprise, knowledge of our misfortune had preceded us, and instead of meeting a scowling farmer we met a very sympathetic one who at once offered the use of the station free of any charge. He directed us to a lumber yard where we made a deal for all the material we needed for rebuilding the trailer.

My father immediately set to rebuilding the trailer, while my brother-in-law and myself worked day and night selling books. We sold enough books not only to pay for the material but also for our keep during those six weeks we were stalled there. Besides, when we finally left the county we had a fancy balance of $90.00. Instead of appreciating the fine Christian qualities of these good people of Caroline County who had learned of our plight and who generously and sympathetically supported us by buying books from us in almost every home, which they would not have done under ordinary circumstances, we felt kind of heroic thinking we had "put one over on the Egyptians," to use Watchtower double talk (Exod. 11:2), taking spoils from them. This was unfortunately the general attitude of most Pioneers and those of the congregations who went out working in those years.

I have now given a running account of some of the highlights of our early experiences as Pioneers. They were not extraordinary. We had them in common with all Pioneers who lasted through this entire Watchtower Intermezzo. The Pioneers were an intrepid group of men and women, who, while not Pioneers for Christianity, were the true Pioneers of the coming Watchtower Theocracy of 1938. They laid the groundwork for the most totalitarian Organization which was ever spawned in liberty-living America and upon our freedom-loving soil! The idea of a Theocracy did not originate in America. It originated in Palestine, was used again in Rome, then perfected in twentieth century garb in Magdeburg.

■The Pioneers Are Demoted

I seemed to have been born to be a Theocratic stooge. Not only did I get inveigled in Magdeburg; but when I broke free, of all things I had to become tied up with the Pioneers who unwittingly became the mainstay of the Theocracy here in America. But as the sinews of Organization in the framework of the congregations grew in strength, and as book sales declined, there came also the slow decline in importance of the Pioneer ranks.

As early as 1935, it was becoming increasingly clear to the Society that its books no longer could be sold as an adjunct to the witnessing work. We were learning the truth of what Abraham Lincoln once said, "You can fool some of the people all of the time, and all of the people some of the time, but you cannot fool all of the people all of the time." We were beginning to find in the rural and small town sections of the country that people were beginning to catch on to our real reason for selling books. Here and there were people who continued buying books, but they were in the minority and these placements would never take care of our operating expenses.

It may be interjected here that we carefully recorded the names and addresses of those who continued to buy books. This list proved very helpful later, during World War II, when the Watchtower Society established the Special Pioneer service to work in smaller cities, paying the workers a special allowance of $25.00 a month. This service in about five years was responsible for establishing more than a thousand Companies of Jehovah's Witnesses.

It was at the Columbus, Ohio, Convention of 1937 that in his address the Judge finally cut loose from the Pioneers. While still praising them, he told them that they were not "the whole works," that others were doing good work too, and implied that they should not take a back seat. Using the Scripture, "Thou hast been faithful over a city, and I shall put thee over ten," the Society appointed many of them Zone servants, and others Company servants. Still others eventually became Special Pioneers during the war years. Most of them eventually found their way into the Watchtower College of Gilead to be trained for missionary work.

■ Doctrinal Developments

The doctrinal development within the Watchtower Organization here in America from 1927 to 1931 was to a great extent a repetition of what had previously taken place in Germany. However, there was none of the directness employed which I described in our approach to the task in Germany. The American personality would not stand for it. More subtle means had to be used.

The study of the pure Word of God had to be set aside among those whom the Watchtower coveted to become its Kingdom Publishers. This was done by cleverly shifting the weight and burden of Scriptural truths into the field of generalities, thereby creating a new and broader meaning of the Scriptures, which they glibly called "New Truths."

Once the concept of spiritbegetting through medium of the Bible was replaced by the idea of the begetting of a new faith based on Watchtower doctrines, the intended transition had been made. The articles of faith for such converts were the voluminous books published in those years at the rate of one each year. This constant bombardment gradually forced that kind of new thinking to come out of the mouth as the "Kingdom Message." The result of the Watchtower procedure was just as intended. All who were subverted began to get exactly the same slant on Bible teachings as feigned by Watchtower verbiage. They began to think alike, talk alike, and witness alike.

Thus the years then from 1926 to 1938 were well employed to create a broad backdrop of deeply echeloned Watchtower doctrine which was so planned, devised, organized and interlocked, that the Society's adherents could secure their nourishment and sustenance only from a continuous flow of *Watchtower* magazines from the Brooklyn presses. In this way the Watchtower Society fulfilled to the rank and file the paternal role of "The Faithful and Wise Servant" providing "food in due season." Without the regular issues of the *Watchtower* magazine, Jehovah's Witnesses would soon starve to inertia and death. While this is a formidable source of strength to the Organization, it also presents a real weakness. Take away the Watchtower Society, its editorial committee and *Watchtower* magazine for any significant length of time, and the Organization will disintegrate. While they built in these years a position of strength for themselves, they have also laid themselves wide open to disintegration if properly, circumspectly and consistently attacked.

Significant in this connection was the appearance of the book *Government* (1928). It was a masterpiece of feigned words laying the groundwork for the future Theocratic structure. It clearly pictured the coming of a "Dictatorship of the Theocracy," presaging what eventually would happen within the ranks of Jehovah's Witnesses and what actually did happen from 1938 on, and what may happen tomorrow to the whole world. In clear and precise forms, through voluminous argumentation, this book set the stage for the coming Theocracy and directed the trend of thought toward the acceptance of a top-down dictatorship.

❖ eleven ❖

DOCTRINAL GYRATIONS

In this phase of my discussion I will give you a summary of the entire theological structure, if you want to call it that, of the Watchtower system. This will save you months of wading through the labyrinth of Watchtower mysteries, and show you what steps were taken to break down Christian truth and what steps were taken to build up Theocratic Watchtower truths. Your head may whirl a bit as you read these pages. Well, so did ours.

■ The Concept of the Beast

Have you ever thoughtfully read the 13th chapter of the book of Revelation? This is the chapter which speaks of the beast which blasphemes and makes war with the saints, as well as of the image of the beast. It speaks of the time to come when no man will be permitted to buy or sell save he that has the mark of the beast on his right hand and in the forehead.

Jehovah's Witnesses hold and proclaim that from the publication of the pamphlet *The Fall of Babylon* on Christendom has constituted the Beast of Revelation 13. Revealed concurrently was Protestantism as the daughters of the Beast. In time the Beast will be perpetuated in a union of Protestants, Catholics, and Jews, which will finally enter into an alliance with the worldly powers. In the end this body, "the Beast," will be overshadowed and overreached by the world power. Then will eventuate the terrible but purifying Battle of Armageddon, in which the Beast will finally be destroyed.

That is an interesting interpretation, and I once accepted it. But now that by God's grace my eyes have been opened I see a much closer parallel to the Beast of Revelation 13 in the Watchtower Organization itself. The Watchtower Society (even as the beast) was "wounded to death" (Rev. 13:3) with the decease of Charles T. Russell, when eventually the Watchtower Society was dissolved and its officers committed to serve in Atlanta. Its deadly wound was healed (Rev. 13:3) with the accession of Judge Rutherford, returning from jail in 1919. In the Theocracy of 1938 the Organization had become so powerful as to rain "fire from heaven" (Rev. 13:13) in the form of pronouncements "of new light" and "new plagues" from the Watchtower Temple. In the columns of the *Watchtower* they reinterpreted the ten plagues (see *Light I* and *II*) which they were sending upon the "religionists." And to be sure no one may worship within the Watchtower Society who does not think as the Society dictates (mark of the beast on the forehead), and does exactly perform as the Society prescribes (mark of the beast on the right hand). This parallel is so striking to me who lived with the Organization for thirty years that I just cannot get away from it. This is what I will mean when from time to time I refer to the Beast and the image of the Beast in connection with the Watchtower Society.

▪ The Book "Life"

You will recall how the Bible Students had emphasized the issue of Israel and eagerly anticipated the return of the princes in 1925. From 1922 on the leaders of the Watchtower Society had fanned this expectation to a white heat. For a time they successfully masked their ulterior aim of using this 1925 expectation as the starting point for expansion. They even sent one of their representatives from Brooklyn to Palestine on the very first ship flying the Israeli flag. Upon his return he told wonderful tales about the return of the Jews to their promised land. This entire topic was used as a basis for the book entitled *Life* (1929), which showed that the end was surely near because the Jews were returning to Palestine.

As the book's red cover had augured, it was but a red herring and its premises were soon discarded by the Society. Its sole purpose was to exploit to the best advantage of the Society the great expectation of 1925. It was intended to effect the change in doctrine which was already reflected in practice in the expanding of the tools of production within sight of the Bible Students, even as the promised year was drawing near. Thus was ushered in a period of flux and change which marked the death of the Bible Students and the birth of Jehovah's Witnesses. Discarding the premise of the book *Life,* only a year after its publication, the attention was redirected from Israel of the flesh now gathering in Palestine to Jehovah's Witnesses, who now became the "spiritual Israelites."

From now on the high Watchtower of the Organization claimed the total benefits of the Jewish nation on a spiritual sphere, appropriating to itself all the prophecies given to the Jews. From henceforth, the issues of the *Watchtower* were utilized for a rewriting of the entire Old Testament into Watchtower verbiage, claiming a fulfillment of the Old Testament prophecies in Jehovah's Witnesses.

In taking over the Old Testament prophecies, in adopting the structure of the Jewish Theocracy, and even in assuming the name of Jehovah's Witnesses (which Isaiah shows in Isaiah 43:10, was the name given to Israel), the Watchtower reversed the advance of Bible truth and returned to things of old. This already presaged how in the course of events it would also retreat from Christianity and its forward focus toward the end of the world, by creating a lower and broader base for mass organization, "the vine of the earth."

From now on, Jehovah's Witnesses were to consider themselves the Israel of God. They would become the chosen people on the "inside" of God's Organization, in the same sense the Jews had felt they were. Their attitude toward those on the "outside" became first patronizing, and finally contemptuous, just as had been the attitude of the Jews toward the Gentiles. This change of thinking brought about by the mechanics of Watchtower feeding was soon to make itself felt in the uncouth and uncivil behavior of Jehovah's Witnesses everywhere. At the same time that they without warrant lay claim to all the blessings and promises of Israel, they also absorbed bigoted, shortsighted, stiff-necked characteristics of the Israel of old.

■ Classes Justified

Another significant book appeared in these doctrinal formative years entitled *Preservation* (1932). Once more characteristically feigning words of Scripture, the Watchtower laid the doctrinal basis for the evolvement of classes within the Organization, in order to eliminate the Christian doctrine of the individual fructification by the Holy Spirit.

In this instance the Watchtower made use of the Scriptural accounts of the lives of Mordecai-Naomi class. It showed how many of the old Bible Students had become unfaithful to the Society. The deflection of many of the original adherents left large gaps and made room for a younger and newer class. It was in relation to the new class that the older class had the name "Mordecai-Naomi class" applied to it. In the Bible drama it was Mordecai who introduced Esther, and Naomi who introduced Ruth into the circle of the faithful. In this case they are given the credit for introducing this new class, namely the "Ruth-Esther class." So, these two names, the Mordecai-Naomi class and the Ruth-Esther class, were not too illogical, were they? In fact, it really makes sense—if you are not squeamish about misusing Scripture.

So far, so good. But more and more it became evident that others were emerging who did not fit into the descriptions of either the Mordecai-Naomi class, or the Ruth-Esther class. Since the Watchtower Organization was scouring the earth for proselytes, many were coming in who cared not at all for spiritual things. Well, something like this had happened before. The Israelites of old had much the same experience in connection with the Gibeonites at the time of their occupation of the land of Palestine, and with the Jehonadabs in later years in the days of Jehu. These had sought shelter with the people of God for the sake of material benefits, peace of mind and physical security. So also numerous newcomers in the insecure years of the twentieth century liked the sense of security which was afforded them by a mere association with something so positive as was the Watchtower Organization, and that without the stress and strain demanded by the Christian life and without conscience to tantalize them. The activities required by the Watchtower Society they could very easily perform: reporting a few hours of work, selling a few books, attending a few meetings where all the thinking was already done for them.

This was what the Society had been working for. That was why they had rewritten the Bible to suit their purposes in their books and magazines, and why they had devised this new mass feeding technique with fornightly issues of Organization provender. This campaign had raised a class which now was coming in in masses, and soon was to come in by the millions. But this caught the Watchtower Society on the horns of a dilemma. They had always taught that the Christ consisted only of 144,000 members. Then what were these millions who were now coming in? Israel of old, whose place the Watchtower and Jehovah's Witnesses had appropriated to themselves, had the same problem. God solved it for Israel of old. The Watchtower had to devise their own solution. But, again they were equal to it.

The Watchtower solution was a lowering of the sights of the Organization. They already had been working on a new norm back there in 1925, when they began to teach that development of individual character was superfluous, and should be replaced by the broader concept of Watchtower Publisher. All that was necessary was to fulfill certain requirements which were in no way spiritual. They were purely carnal or businesslike, consisting of recording and reporting time, selling books and attending meetings. So they already had the solution to this problem of the unspiritual multitude waiting in the background. Soon they would grasp it firmly with both hands; once they did, what a change it made in the composition of the Watchtower Organization!

Up to this time Bible Students believed that those proving unfaithful in attaining the goal of the higher calling in this age, but who were spiritbegotten since that is the only way one can come into relationship with God through Jesus Christ, would receive a brief second chance during the Millennium. Now the Watchtower Society had to change this interpretation, and show that this great multitude was not a spiritual class after all, but was an earthly class.

Well, that was easy. Did not the Psalmist say "the earth is the footstool of God's throne"? If then, so they argued, this class will find a place not *on* but *before* the throne, it follows they must be earthly. Therefore they are actually an unspiritual class coming to life in the Kingdom on earth, as had the Jonadabs been alive amidst the Jewish Theocracy. However, a study of Revelation 7 will not only effectively debunk this particular argument, but give a vivid example of the type of the misuse of Scripture regularly employed by the Watchtower Society.

The books *Preparation* (1933) and *Riches* (1934) were issued to present and summarize these new doctrines and their formulation, and to engender the necessary motivation within the rank and file to undertake the tasks which the Watchtower Society had planned for them. Not only was there the need for making room for a new class, but also the need for creating the impression of the seemingly higher spiritual plateau than the one the Society now sought to relinquish. It must never be said that Jehovah's Witnesses had to lower their sights, as they had so often gloatingly pointed out that the Catholics had done for practical considerations! This change, therefore, had to be presented very carefully and very adroitly to the rank and file.

■Incorporating the Gibeonites

Let us note in a bit more detail how they cleverly made use of the Scriptural picture of the Gibeonites.

The Gibeonites, as you will remember, were the inhabitants of a Canaanite city lying in the pathway of Israel's occupation of the Promised Land. Long before Joshua and the Israelites approached the environs of the city, these

good people sent a deputation to Joshua pledging subjection and asking in exchange a pledge of protection. The
Gibeonites made it appear as if they had come from a far
distant country. It was not until after a treaty of peace had
been duly made and ratified that it was discovered that
the Gibeonites had tricked Joshua. Israel reluctantly honored the treaty, and allowed the Gibeonites to dwell in
their midst and to share their blessings. It even fought a
battle for them against the Canaanites. But Israel did not
integrate the Gibeonites into itself. Instead it made of them
slaves, or "hewers of wood and carriers of water" as the
Scriptural account puts it. (See Josh. 9:3–27; 10:6–10.)
The Gibeonites gladly accepted this role in exchange for
the benefits which it afforded. It is this event which the
Watchtower Society culled out of the history of Israel in
order to justify and interpret the role which it planned for
the Jonadabs, or unspiritual "Great Multitude" within its
midst. This story adapted itself admirably to the Society's
purpose—even though anyone not already in the Watchtower clutches and hypnotized by the Watchtower jargon
will have a hard time to see the connection.

So a way was designed for the multitude of newcomers to live within the "New Nation." It no longer mattered
that they were not "spiritbegotten." They could dwell
within the framework of God's Organization as slaves, as
modern "hewers of wood and carriers of water," so to
speak.

What a vista for increase was opened up here for the
Watchtower by virtue of this explanation! The Watchtower
Society correctly saw that this new class was present by
the millions throughout the land of the anti-typical
Canaanites, namely Christendom. But the book, *Preparation* (1933), shows this would not only be limited to Christendom. So, here the Watchtower Society was laying the
groundwork: first for the emergence of a vast unspiritual
class out of the lands of Christendom; and then later, for

the emergence of a still larger class to come out of the pagan nations, a class which never so much as laid claim to the spirituality of Christianity. Thus naturally would the Jonadabs become "the Great Multitude."

■ Christianity Discarded

The Watchtower Society had now reached a point where it was forced to go even further. Quietly and imperceptibly it now had to disrobe itself of the mantle of Christianity which it so long had worn for a cover and disguise. This was necessary if it were to be at all successful among the discontented masses within Christendom and later of Christ-hating heathendom. So the Watchtower Society set about to bring a change in its designation or name. "The only name under heaven by which men can be saved" had become an impediment to the "progress" of the New World Society. Looking back into their blueprint of the formation of Israel of old, in the Old Testament, they soon hit upon the idea of calling themselves after the name of Jehovah, "Jehovah's Witnesses." They failed to realize that in thus seeking to shed all connection with Christ they were also branding themselves as opposers of Him who had provided for Christ's first appearance on earth for man's redemption.

Twelve years of "the second tier" of the Watchtower Society (as I term the new setup) had elapsed since 1919. The Society grasped this occasion to nail down its newly adopted doctrines and practices by issuing a three-volume commemorative publication entitled *Vindication* (1932).

Even though the Society had by this time disowned the name of Christ, it did not think it inconsistent to make use of one of Christ's parables to further its purpose. In fact, it saw real advantage in doing so. It could give Christian color to its argument. It found a parable which was admirably adapted for its misuse, namely, the parable of The Laborers in the Vineyard. It compared the twelve years since 1919 to the twelve hours of the parable. All the laborers in the Organization were to receive an equal reward, regardless of the length or type of service. And what reward was that to be? Why, the wonderful new name, "Jehovah's Witnesses."

This parable served their purpose wonderfully well. The Organization even had the counterpart of the murmurers of the parable. They were the older ones, or rather, the ones who had worked the longer. These were those of the Mordecai-Naomi class, which had with some of the new Ruth-Esther class turned aside in disappointment and dissatisfaction. But all without exception and without distinction, even those newly come in as unspiritual Jonadabs, would now have one designation. The spiritual and unspiritual alike would be comprehended under the one name "Jehovah's Witnesses." Herewith the parable had served its purpose.

But in order to bring forth the intended multitudes from out of Christendom, and later from heathendom, the Organization had to make a name for itself. The best way to accomplish this purpose was to go to war! It is surprising how well and how long the Scriptural glory of the Gibeonites served the Watchtower purpose. The Society now, as had Israel of old, went to war in behalf of its adopted "Gibeonites." It carried the battle for "freedom of worship" all the way from the Justice of the Peace to the Supreme Court. Throughout the battle the Society feigned the role of martyr and underdog, and emerged as a victorious hero. The campaign was 100 percent successful. The details of this battle will be told in subsequent pages.

Yes, the Watchtower organization had stooped—and had conquered!

✧ twelve ✧

STRATEGY PAYS OFF

■ Status in the Early Thirties

The Watchtower leaders had now perfected the means for a rigid, top-down control of the entire Organization. Through their books, booklets and the *Watchtower* magazines, they had forged a doctrinal straight jacket. This generated a kind of thinking called "Organization Mindedness," a new intellectual lever which we in Germany back in 1926 had called *gleichschaltung*. This was couched in regular forms of study: the Sunday Bible lectures had been replaced by the cut-and-dried *Watchtower* studies with cut-and-dried questions, and cut-and-dried answers. The prayer and experience meeting had given way to the Service meeting in which the Society's instructions were the sole topic of discussion, with weekly reviews and arrangements for local application. Home Bible study was discontinued for Book Studies, with the Society's books and textbooks in the place of the Bible, and the Bible relegated to a position where it was restricted almost exclusively to reference use.

Such books as *Light I* and *II* (1928) describing Revelation with the new Watchtower slant, and *Vindication I, II* and *III* and *Religion* assailed every concept ever taught in Christianity and attacked many practices civilized men of the past 2,000 years have painstakingly evolved. In endeavoring to create a super-state, or a spiritual extraterritoriality, these books and other booklets branded the demand for licenses to sell books in towns as illegal and improper, branded the saluting of the flag of a country as idol worship, branded the removing of the hat in common politeness in the presence of a lady as creature worship, and branded a thousand and one things we accept as common usage today as unscriptural.

This history strikingly established the truth of the principle that departure from Scripture has consequences. First of all they had given up the Scriptural position that all brethren in Christ are of equal standing before the Lord. After this departure they soon reached the point of which Paul writes to Timothy, "For the time will come when they will not endure sound doctrine; but having itching ears, will heap to themselves teachers after their own lusts; and will turn away their ears from the truth, and turn aside to fables" (2 Tim. 4:3).

How true this all proved to be in the case of the Watchtower slaves. Each of the classes—the Mordecai-Naomi, the Ruth-Esther and the Jonadab classes—had itching ears to hear all the good they could about their own class and all the bad they could about the other classes. Naturally, only a superior set of teachers could serve a bill of fare which would satisfy each class in particular and all classes in general. This made the Faithful and Wise Servant class virtually indispensable and raised them to a high level of importance. And this superior class was not slow to grasp every opportunity to pit class against class in rivalry to merit favor and standing in the Organization.

Outwardly they still continued to accuse Christendom of being divisive. Vociferously they threw into the teeth of the Christians Paul's injunction to the Corinthians, "Is

Christ divided?" But in practice they themselves were divided right down the middle: Remnant and Jonadab. Then the Remnant in turn was divided into the Mordecai-Naomi and Ruth-Esther classes, and the Jonadabs into "people of goodwill," Jonadabs and the Great Multitude—all fine shades of differences. Organizationally they were stratified into Directors of the Society and the charter members; then Bethelites and Servants to the brethren and branch Servants; then company Servants and the common leg men, or Kingdom Publishers. Of course, this is an oversimplification. And all this time indoctrination was progressively affecting what can be called goosestep thinking, and Organization instructions were bringing about goosestep action.

■Martyrdom with a Purpose

While the printed media gushing forth from Brooklyn carried with it a stream of new indoctrination brainwashing fluids, we noticed three developments which were forcing a major policy change. First of all, books could no longer be sold in large quantities by merely going from house to house with them and offering them for a contribution. People were refusing to give contributions. Next, it became evident that some sensational method was necessary to establish the new name of "Jehovah's Witnesses." In order to gain attention it was necessary to create a condition of war through the creation of issues, coupled with an appearance of being persecuted. The point had been reached where everything that had been written in the books *Preparation* and *Religion* was to be put into practice.

It now became the studied policy of the Watchtower Society to make Jehovah's Witnesses hated of all men—by their way of preaching, by the methods of their preaching and by what they were preaching. They hoped thus to put themselves in the position where they appeared to be martyrs for the sake of religion. It is for this reason they instituted Sunday witnessing parties. These they likened, using the terminology of Revelation as interpretation in the book *Light,* as "Locusts eating off the varnish of the Religionists."

In order to wage an effective campaign, they decided to concentrate on an area conveniently near to Brooklyn. The State of New Jersey presented itself as a convenient area in which to be "thrown to the lions"—and, they hoped, to martyrdom. Dotted with many small exclusive communities, this area held a population which liked to spend its Sundays in peace and tranquility. Upon them descended these "witnessing parties" on Sundays.

Complaints soon poured into the Mayor's and the Police Chief's office, sometimes hundreds at a time. When the police accused the witnesses and asked them for their license to peddle books, they naturally refused to secure them. Sensing martyrdom, they now came back oftener than they would have done otherwise. Having failed in the attempt to regulate the coming and going of these witnesses, the city fathers framed ordinances prohibiting bookselling without a license and leveled fines. In doing so they were stepping into the trap which the Watchtower had cleverly baited.

Meanwhile the Society was perfecting its Organization in preparation for the battles which it so clearly foresaw. It organized the Jehovah's Witnesses into divisions composed of about fifteen companies, each in a compact homogenous area. This divisional setup would make possible quick, organized mass action. Divisional defense funds were established for the coming battles. In this manner the Society readied New Jersey to be the proving grounds for mass action practices. It was to develop a technique to be employed everywhere in the future.

The authorities, harassed by irate and panicky citizens, played right into the hands of the Witnesses by making the initial arrests. Once that occurred, the Witnesses came back again and again, courting mass arrests and mass sentences, which they immediately appealed. The Society could have put a speedy halt to the litigation by appealing to the principle of freedom of the press. Instead, it insisted on using the freedom of religion approach. The Society realized that the longer this issue was kept alive, the more was to be gained in the end. The courts continued to hold that Jehovah's Witnesses were not being denied the freedom of worship, that they were not being molested in their worship in the Kingdom Halls, etc. They would even be allowed to sell books if they obtained licenses.

By their very audacity the Jehovah's Witnesses irritated the courts to a point where they gave them their desired martyrdom in the form of fines and jail sentences. In this way the Jehovah's Witnesses made it appear as if they were being arrested, tried and convicted for practicing their religion. They then raised a loud cry of intolerance, even though they themselves had repeatedly and openly declared, "Religion is a snare and a racket!" By use of mass action with divisional backing they on many occasions resorted to mob violence, literally saturating a town until the jails were filled. Then they would pound away at the authorities.

We knew all along that we had a right to distribute our books, booklets and pamphlets without censorship under the freedom of the press section of the Bill of Rights. We refrained from using it, because our present methods were drawing fire and were giving us the desired martyrdom. This had tremendous advertising value and was creating sympathy for us.

■It Worked

These court battles accomplished everything desired of them. The constant jar of discrimination against a minority group slowly brought about the formation of a new group of people in the land, who, upon hearing and reading about these battles, began to read the many books of Jehovah's Witnesses which they had purchased in former years. These also purchased the new books, which at every turn were presented to them, and subscribed by the hundreds of thousands to the *Consolation* and the *Watchtower* magazines. This gave the bookselling campaign a shot in the arm, and publications were once again accepted upon payment of a contribution.

These battles accomplished another important purpose. The Watchtower Society and Jehovah's Witnesses appeared as the magnanimous champions of what they adroitly called "the people of good will." The Jonadabs now appeared in full view as a mass. And to them the Society hammered home by means of one-sided reports in its magazines and books and booklets, that a great battle was being waged in behalf of their rights and their freedom of worship. All this was buttressed in the public press by free publicity concerning the arrest, trials and convictions. And how wonderfully the analogy of the Gibeonites again held! The Society carefully explained that they had risen to the defense of the Jonadabs exactly in the same manner as had Joshua and the Israelites in the battle with the Canaanite armies in defense of Gibeon. And as from that day on the Gibeonites had become Israel's slaves, or "hewers of wood and carriers of water," so now the Jonadab class became Watchtower Slaves.

■"It May Be Ye Shall Be Hid in the Day of His Anger"

It was taken for granted that the multitude now entering no longer were "begotten of the Spirit." They were

Jonadabs, who had come into the Organization to escape the approaching storm of Armageddon, which could break out almost any minute. They came in order to find protection in the city of refuge, or the Theocracy. They were carefully taught that if they stayed close within the confines of the Organization, and did not stray out of it, followed all its instructions religiously, listened attentively to Watchtower indoctrination, went out as Publishers regularly and rigidly reported the time they spent in doing so, then *maybe* they would be saved in Armageddon.

This "maybe salvation," in contrast to our certainty as Christians, was driven home by quoting to them Zephaniah 2:3, "Seek ye Jehovah, all ye meek of the earth, that have kept his ordinances; seek righteousness, seek meekness: it may be ye shall be hid in the day of His anger."

Of course, the Watchtower's use of this emphatic call to self-examination was a misinterpretation and perversion of the text. However, it served the purpose—and that was all that really mattered. It kept the Jonadabs looking to the Watchtower as their possible way of escape in the impending Armageddon.

But the Watchtower's misinterpretation of this text did more. It eloquently proclaimed to all who had ears to hear the fact that the Society was not a Christian organization. For, if it were Christian it could have and would have promised safety with certainty to all who turned to the Lord in true repentance. All it could promise was a *maybe* escape from a trumped up danger.

▪Split Personality

During this period new methods of publishing and witnessing were being tested. All was gradually brought onto a mass production basis. Gone was the individual training of the individual Bible Student who daily studied God's

Word, and depended upon the work of the Holy Spirit. Indoctrination was taking the place of Bible study. Since the Jehovah's Witnesses were not allowed to do their own spiritual thinking as they were guided by the Holy Spirit, they became incapable of carrying on Christian warfare by effectively wielding the sword of the Spirit, which is the Word of God (Eph. 6:17).

■The Testimony Card

As a result we have the origin of the familiar testimony card prepared at headquarters. The Witness could present this card to the householder in explanation of the current book offer, as does the deaf mute in an effort to sell his wares.

Ostensibly this gadget was prepared to help the Publisher sell more books. Actually it had a far more sinister purpose. The Society realized that the new class of Kingdom Publishers and Jonadabs really knew very little of the Scriptures. The Society leaders felt that the testimony card would cover up this ignorance, at the same time that it helped the sale of books. Furthermore, the testimony card served as a bridle for those older ones who were quite capable of wielding "the sword of the Spirit, which is the Word of God," and gave evidence of the work of the Holy Spirit. In this case the testimony card served the purpose of a straight jacket, and finally, "quenched the Spirit" in the case of those who submitted to this gimmick.

This testimony card was a vicious thing with pathetic results. During World War II, when I accompanied conscientious objectors to examination boards where hearings were held to determine the validity of their claim of being ministers, I realized to my consternation that most of such Jonadabs were incapable of answering even the most rudimentary questions about the Bible. One board member once said, "You mean to tell me that you are a minister and cannot tell me where to find this passage of Scripture?" "We do not use this method of preaching. We use a testimony card," cockily replied the Jonadab.

That testimony card graphically showed the nadir to which a whole people had sunk who had once prided themselves in their Scriptural acumen and knowledge. Instead of being begotten "with the word of truth" (James 1:18), the Jonadabs were begotten of the Theocratic spirit of a mass organization, by seeds other than the word of God, mass seeds of Watchtower books, booklets and magazines. With feigned words the Society had made merchandise of them, as the apostle Peter had warned. Since their viewpoint emanated entirely from the opinions and conclusions which they read in the Society's publications, their brain became totally washed of any other ideas they might ever have loosely held about the Bible, themselves or other people. Their own thoughts were thus replaced by a narrow sphere or circumscribed area of thought, or as the Watchtower put it, a "channel." They became "Organization minded."

Jonadabs had only one purpose in going out, and that was like robots or automatons to say, "I represent the Watchtower," and hand over the testimony card. Then they would show the book and place it, and collect the contribution. After they had done that for a spell, they would go home, sit down and mechanically make out a time report and placement report on a form supplied them by the Company servant. That was the full extent of their religious responsibility and constituted for them "the reasonable service" which Paul discusses for a Christian in Romans 12. Jehovah's Witnesses, by virtue of the success of the well laid plans of the Faithful and Wise Servant Class in Brooklyn now were but class robots. The testimony card and the daily report slip were the height of individual freedom *allowed* them.

All this has resulted in the sorry state of affairs we witness among Jehovah's Witnesses today. By constant repression of mind and heart, they have become mentally and emotionally sick. They have delusions of persecution and Armageddon tremors. They carry a permanent chip on their shoulder, and are incapable of appreciating any one of all the rest of mankind on the face of this wide, wide earth. Everything is "channelized" to them from the Brooklyn Watchtower. There is not a jot or a tittle of their own individuality in a carload of books they sell. They have become prisoners in a modern snake pit.

✤ thirteen ✤

UPHELD
BY THE COURTS

■ Suspicions Aroused

As the worldwide campaign to sell the Watchtower books, booklets and magazines continued, there were those who began to recognize it for the racket which it was. Officials and other groups were beginning to suspect that perhaps the enormous sales of this Watchtower merchandise and religious goods under the guise of practicing religion, were no more than business sales without a license. Here and there articles in the press and in magazines raised questions. There was, for instance, in the year 1940 an article by Stanley High, in the *Saturday Evening Post* entitled, "Armageddon, Inc." Being subjected to this sort of publicity, the Watchtower High Command had to counteract.

The Watchtower Society knew that the opposition came from those who were basically religious and valued religious freedom. In designing countermoves to destroy the growing impression that the Watchtower campaign was a racket, the Society took this fact into account. Whenever

Jehovah's Witnesses were arrested for selling books without a license, legal action was immediately begun to establish that this was merely preaching by use of the printed page instead of the spoken word. This claim of religious freedom as a justification for their practices was repeated again and again, despite numerous defeats. They were much too astute to give up this chain of court trials and subsequent convictions, arrests and rearrests, and mass actions followed by still more arrests.

This surefire pattern served its purpose well. It slowly but surely began to create the impression that the Jehovah's Witnesses were being persecuted for practicing their "religion," and the accusation that they were conducting a racket gradually fell away. At the same time the Organizational leaders hoped that they were now beginning to realize the fondest dream of the Watchtower Society, to be recognized as the religion of the land and then of the whole world.

This dream was first visualized by the Judge, during his arrest and subsequent conviction and the dissolution of the Society. This was and remains the goal toward which the whole Organization gravitates, which is, to make the whole world a New World Society. They knew that they could ride a long way toward this goal on the widespread innate sympathy for the underdog. Before this campaign started the people had begun to refuse to buy books any longer in ordinary house-to-house work. Now many again became interested if for no other reason than to support Jehovah's Witnesses in the fight.

How this actually worked out in practice is illustrated by an experience I had while witnessing in Plainfield, New Jersey. I had just left one house, having placed two bound books there, when I noticed a police car moving slowly toward the curb. The officers called to me, but I pretended that I did not hear them. I proceeded to the porch of the next house. A man watching from the window quickly opened the door for me even before I knocked, and I entered. I thus got unsolicited aid in foiling the attempt of the police to arrest me. My benefactor invited me to sit down and expressed his chagrin over the police. He bought four books from me, giving me a dollar contribution, and allowed me to stay the whole hour required for the police to get tired and leave. I finished the street unhindered, placing more than twenty books there.

■ "Religion Is a Snare and a Racket"

It is amazing how often and how successfully the Watchtower Society changed its tactics to suit the occasion and purpose. At the same time that it was ostensibly putting forth every effort to have the Supreme Court of the United States declare its selling practices as a proper exercise of religious rights, it set out on a course which seemed diametrically opposed and contradictory. The Watchtower Society cleverly throughout the land raised the organized cry, "Religion is a snare and a racket." Thus by accusing others it drew away from itself the charge that its bookselling campaign was a racket. Soon Jehovah's Witnesses paraded up and down streets with sandwich signs attached to their persons advertising this slogan, "Religion is a snare and a racket." They claimed *they* were giving something in kind for the money received, but that *religion* gives nothing for money given to it; or, as the Judge put it, religion "gives only husks."

This new ruse soon had the desired effect. The furor it created brought about a revulsion against them by many of the more religious minded, and gave rise to widespread mob violence. This forced the police who previously had been so busy arresting them, to turn around and protect them from harm. Jehovah's Witnesses played their part well. They ceased fighting and surrendered themselves to mob violence, arrests, court trials, boycotts, loss of jobs. Thus Jehovah's Witnesses created for themselves the status of a persecuted minority based on the practice of their religion. As a result of all this the entire policy of the Watchtower Society of selling books and starting companies of Jehovah's Witnesses in all the cities of the land now received a mighty forward push.

But finally the condition of warfare was spreading so rapidly and was increasing in intensity to such a degree that it threatened to get out of hand. This was the signal for the Society to use the proper legal approach to get favorable court action. It finally appealed to its right of freedom of the press. And it already had all the courts on its side as a result of its giving the impression of being a religious minority under persecution.

The Society moved into the picture of Griffin, Georgia. It appealed the Lovell case there to the higher courts, and finally all the way to the Supreme Court of the United States. Court, as might have been expected, held that the books and booklets which Jehovah's Witnesses were distributing were products of a free press and their distribution was protected by the Constitution of the United States, unmolestedly by city ordinances and licenses.

This Lovell vs. Griffin case was the first victory of Jehovah's Witnesses, but by no means the last. In fact, it was but the beginning of a long saga of writing into the law of the land the legality of all the practices of Jehovah's Witnesses.

The Society lost no opportunity to declare the extent of its victory! If you will read Watchtower literature from 1936 on, you will see how they lay claim to miraculous deeds done in their behalf by God. In fact, they glory that God used the enemy to establish the Organization, or the second Watchtower tier.

Now that Jehovah's Witnesses had been given the status of an established religion, and their religious practice of selling books had been declared a proper religious exercise, they needed actual places of worship like those of the other religions. After all, they had to put up a proper front. Kingdom Halls were the answer.

Now that they had legal backing, they stepped up their bid for mass attention from any and all who would listen. There was room in the Organization for all. The Christian concept of spiritbegetting as a selective standard had long been abandoned. Anyone could easily become a Jehovah's Witness! All they had to do was to become a Kingdom Publisher, go out from house to house, sell books and report regularly the placements made and the time spent, and turn in the contributions. And all their thinking was to be brought into complete harmony with that of the Watchtower Society by reading of the Watchtower magazine and the books, and studying them in area studies and Kingdom Halls.

▪ Consolidating the Gains

These victories of the ruling core first within the Organization, and then without in the field of the world, firmly established the Faithful and Wise Servant Class. The Watchtower Society had now reached the dizzy Theocratic pinnacle where it was absolutely impervious to opposition and criticism within the Organization. It took full advantage of its position. If any of Jehovah's Witnesses did not cooperate 100 percent in receiving "truths" and instructions from headquarters, then the Society would no longer deal with them, nor give them anything to do, nor dispense any favors to them. Thus those who were the most faithful to the Society, though their talents might be nil, had the bigger and better jobs handed to them.

As it always did when it was at all possible, the Society operated on an ostensibly Scriptural basis. In this case, it appealed to the Lord's statement, "I say unto you, that unto everyone that hath shall be given; but from him that hath not, even that which he hath, shall be taken from him." It exempted no one from this rule, claiming for itself the power of attorney in distributing the Lord's favor. The Watchtower leaders staunchly contended that as the Faithful and Wise Servant Class, "all goods had been given to them" by the Lord; and they enforced that dictum dictatorially upon all within their midst. If someone was recalcitrant and would not follow instructions or even dared to voice opposition, they wrote him off, figuring that he would be more trouble than help. They generally dropped such a one so abruptly and unceremoniously that he usually did not know what hit him. On the other hand, if someone showed by his amenability to instructions that he was their boy, or "slave" as they put it later, they would entrust him with more and more assignments and responsibilities, thus enhancing his prestige within the Organization.

The Organization in America was finally reaching the point we had already reached in Germany in 1926. At that time we had divided Berlin into forty units. Here now, beginning with New York (which was initially divided into seven units), many of the larger congregations of the land were similarly divided. At first, also as we had done in Berlin, a monthly meeting was held embracing the old congregation. Then gradually the units became independent companies and finally became an integral part of the Zone.

With this historical dissertation before you, coupled with my own eyewitness experience in the Organization during these momentous times, fellow Christian, be stirred up! Your Christian way is at stake! A Theocratic force with tremendous power is bent upon a New World Society. If once it is established it will be a slave society and then it will be too late.

The Watchtower "religion" has been legalized as a religion. And there is no denying the fact that in our twentieth century, with big business and big commerce and big finance, it holds a fatal charm for mankind. Multitudes have heeded the song of the harlot (see Rev. 17:5; Isa. 23:15–17), and sold their individuality. Like the Lorelei of the Rhineland saga, its fatal tune has lured millions into soul death!

✦ fourteen ✦

SERVICE
IN NEW YORK

I will now bring the account of my personal experiences up to date with this narrative.

■ A Case History

By 1935 I was holding a Pioneer assignment in Rensselaer County, New York, just across the Hudson from Albany. Our family worked this large county with acceptable success.

During that time it became quite evident to us that the Company servant at Albany was a man of character. As an old time Bible Student he was not bowing to the Society. I knew that he was skating on thin ice. I was watching this scene with keen interest. From my vantage point across the Hudson I could see the ominous forces of Theocracy gathering about his head. I wondered who would be selected to give him the coup de grace. I hoped not I!

Then one day, there appeared on the scene an elderly brother who was connected with the Society's Service Department. In view of the fact that he had been pensioned, he could devote all his time to getting the Company servant out. Usually that was a delicate and major operation. It had to be done without repercussions from inside the Company.

In this case friction was soon stirred up. When this special brother began getting Society instructions over the head of the duly appointed Company servant it did not take long for the members of the Company to sense who was truly in favor with the Society. In the meanwhile, we had received orders from headquarters to cooperate fully with this man. We stirred up the witnessing activity, and took a leading part in the service. Thus we did our part in creating the desired diversion.

Gradually the incumbent Company servant was forced to take a backseat, and the Society's disfavor with him became quite evident. More and more, because we kept them busy throughout the week, the Publishers rallied around us. Finally the Company servant had enough and resigned. In his place a member of my family was appointed Company servant. Being a staunch and subservient Watchtower Society boy he still holds this position. Thus quietly, while preventing him from leading anybody away from the Company, was this too individualistic Elder defrocked, and replaced by a loyal slave of the Theocracy. The technique has been neatly perfected. It has proved to be surefire, and has been used with success wherever necessary.

▪Far from Infallible

In 1936 I was at my parents' home in New York City, preparing to go back to my assignment in Georgia, where I held a Pioneer territory. I received a call to come to Bethel. I was asked to stay in New York and to become the Company servant for Manhattan. This was much more to my liking than to go back to the South at the time. So I accepted. This acceptance was erroneously construed at headquarters to mean an especial willingness to give up personal plans for theirs. It was interpreted as an indication that I was their boy, and it soon brought me the offer of an advancement. However, that promotion, an offer to enter Bethel, was the last thing I wanted. I wiggled out of it as fast as I could without bringing the whole house down upon me, and getting the cold shoulder permanently from them.

From innumerable other cases, added to mine, I learned that this arbitrary rule by which they advanced people or demoted people, based upon seeming willingness to "eat humble crow," was not a very efficient one to say the least. And it certainly was not as Scriptural as they contended. If the Society had the mind of the Lord, as they claimed, it would not have made the errors of judgment to which it seemed unusually prone, some of which were appalling.

The only reason I mention a few glaring errors made by the Society is to debunk by implication the Society's claim that it has exclusive access to the ear and mind of Jesus Christ. The Society made many serious and often very evident errors in selection of personnel.

Many errors were procedural. I recall an almost ridiculous error made while I was Company servant in Manhattan. I received from the legal desk of the Society a form letter addressed to all Company servants. It designated a day four weeks ahead on which day all Publishers were to nail a certain attack and proclamation against religion on all the doors of the churches in our territory. When I read it, it jarred something in my mind. It just did not sound right to me. Certainly I realized that Dr. Martin Luther had nailed these on the Castle Church doors of Wittenberg; but he almost died for that! After consideration I decided to visit a "man of goodwill" who was a lawyer. Since I had been witnessing to him and was on friendly terms with him I could ask him for an answer to a hypothetical case—without paying a retainer! He pointed out that the pamphlet would not draw legal action against it if it were distributed by hand; it would become libelous, however, in each instance and in every case where it was nailed to a church door. He warned that if the proposed plan were carried out we would draw down upon us nationwide litigation. Upon learning that, I called the Secretary to the Judge and told him about the letter and about my findings. The next day I received another form letter by special delivery (companies farther afield received telegrams) canceling this scheme. From that day on the legal desk was hamstrung. It had committed a stupid blunder.

Many, many such false moves and improper judgments come to mind. But let these few suffice to make the point that the Watchtower Society is far from infallible. It is no more the mouthpiece of the Lord than was Balaam when he pompously addressed himself to Israel (Numbers 22 and 23).

But this Society fully acted as if it was the head of gold of Daniel 2:31–34, divinely inspired and approved. The locally appointed Elders had now completely disappeared and in their place had come representatives of the Society, Company servants holding an official letter of appointment to the position by virtue of the Society's self-assumed Theocratic power. Most of those who were appointed in this manner had no Christian background whatever as had the Elders of the Bible Student era. They had no conception of what constitutes a proper Christian assembly, or ecclesia; and the idea of fellowshipping, which was a major purpose of the assembling of Christians for edification, sounded silly and maudlin to them. To them, as products of a class, and now official appointees of the Faithful and Wise Servant Class, individual Publishers mattered little. All that mattered was to make the classes which were now coming better tools of the Theocracy. Meetings were designed to make these classes better Publishers. As for being better Christians, that never entered the picture!

■My Heart Is Not in It

After a few more months in New York, sometime in the summer of 1936, I was called into the office by the Service Department and asked to stay in the city to become a Unit servant of Manhattan.

I was hesitant about accepting this assignment, since I sensed that my attitude toward the Watchtower Society was undergoing a change. Unfortunately for me, once I had left Magdeburg Bethel behind I had not been able to recapture my individual status as a Christian New Creation, which I had lost when I entered into the Society's offices on August 18, 1924.

The reason I lost and could not recapture my status as an individual Christian is plain to me now. I did not study God's Word as the basic truth but kept on reading the *Watchtower* avidly, as well as the Watchtower published books and booklets. In this way I filled my mind with their provender and could not free myself from Organization mindedness.

But I continued to carry within me a hard core of individuality, which refused to yield. In moments when I was free from the Organizational rat-tat-rat-a-tat, this Christian individuality would assert itself in qualms of conscience. This phenomenon, I noticed, was recurring more often lately. It was bothering me. It gave me a kind of attitude which prevented me from ever again becoming emotionally and spiritually a real part of the Organization. It permitted me at times to stand aloof from it in a sphere of objective detachment, as if I were looking in from the outside. I did not have this experience very often but just once in a while when I relaxed. Most of the time I was far too active to entertain such attitudes. Later, however, I was to be led to freedom because of this ability to be objective about the whole thing.

But now, upon receiving an offer to remain in New York, because it coincided with my personal desire to stay in New York, I accepted. This acceptance did not mean that I had become an obedient slave of the Watchtower Society. That sounds horrible from a Theocratic point of view, and its very statement even here is rank heresy to the ears of Jehovah's Witnesses. But this attitude was the first promise of eventual freedom from the thralldom to the Watchtower Society.

Let me here direct a word to the thousands who today look for escape from their Watchtower slavery. You will first of all have to develop an attitude of "take it or leave it." The ability to dissimulate while in good standing in the Organization is the first step away from it. It has to precede any other moves. Remember, the Society through its pattern of activity set for Publishers, enforces its mark upon your forehead and forearm, and thus makes you work for it. But if you can gradually assume an attitude of objectivity, and work and think of the Theocracy in a detached and increasingly superficial way, it is obvious that the mark of the beast will gradually relinquish its hold on your soul. Instead of a permanent mark it will be but a tattoo which through a simple operation, though painful, can be removed at will in the future. In this manner the Lord caused the mark of the beast on my right hand and on my forehead to be removed—though through painful experiences, as you will note when I discuss the mechanics of my flight to freedom from Watchtower slavery.

∎A Ringside Seat

Here then was an opportunity for me to stay in New York, near Brooklyn, the Bethel of the Watchtower Society, and to watch from a ringside seat what transpired. My body was in the Organization and I was instinctively observing the practices of my overdeveloped Watchtower herd-instinct. But my individuality was becoming strengthened by adverse reaction to being subjected again to something I once before lived through in Germany in building up the work there. It came first in the form of slight revulsion, then a here-we-go-again attitude, then sheer futility. I had a grandstand seat for watching the Organization in action and I was eventually going to have to pay the price for that dissimulation which alone made that grandstand seat tolerable. What a horrible price it was! It was only worth it because it eventually led to freedom! I only hope that in writing about this candidly I can show thousands of my brethren how they too can place themselves in a position where the Word of God may do its work in their hearts. The Lord alone can save their souls from being swallowed up permanently in the worship of the "image of the beast" (Rev. 13).

■ I Get Out of Line

Since I was familiar with the routine as a result of my experience in Germany I was in the enviable position of always being able to anticipate the Organization's moves. It was this which at first got me into trouble on several occasions. As Company servant I began putting some of these anticipated moves into practice. I was soon instructed not to run ahead, but to await the lead of the Organization. Actually I had "erred" deliberately, in order to ascertain whether or not this pattern was being followed on a long range basis. It was. In this way I set events moving which were not so good for me, and which almost cost me my relationship with the Society.

Early in 1937 I received a special delivery letter from the President's office. It asked me to appear at the office for a chat with the President, Judge Rutherford! With my heart filled with misgivings, I set out to see him at the scheduled time.

▪ It Was Torture

Christian, if you have ever enjoyed the peace and happiness of the mind of Christ, a peace which goes beyond understanding, then you will feel with me as I picture for you the torments and tortures I lived through from now on in the Watchtower Hell. Emotions of joy and pain, shades of light and darkness, feelings of ecstasy and torment, alternated in my life from now on.

Here I was, imprisoned in the tightest organization on earth. It was beginning to create in me sensations of frightening claustrophobia. It was becoming evident that I was not one who could be absorbed and brought down to the level of a beast animated by mass instinct. Neither was I ready to act robot fashion according to patterns laid out in Organization instructions. Why? My soul or individuality was still awake and alive; at least, a spark was still there, a modicum of individuality.

I was like in a nightmare, seeing the danger and wanting to flee, but my legs would not move and I could not make good my escape; but neither could the danger catch up with me. Nightmares are usually the result of overeating or eating bad food combinations. I did not know then, but I now know that I was in this state because I was feeding on that which issued from the Brooklyn Watchtower through its policy committee and editorial committee. I no longer fed on the proper fare of a Christian, the word of truth which comes from the mouth of the Lord, or on the manna from Heaven, Christ Jesus.

All this worked against a possible escape from what was becoming an unbearable situation. I was not reading or studying the Bible with an open and unprejudiced mind. Without the comfort and strength and guidance of the Holy Spirit, I was unable to scale the walls of the Watchtower Organization. My new life as a Christian thus was so weak I was not able to walk in the Spirit and get away. Escape I did later, almost eighteen years from the date of the events discussed in this phase of my story, and then only by the grace of God. But before finally coming free I had to drink the very dregs of the cup of the Watchtower wine, a wine which is Theocratic and heady, and which at times not only destroyed my mental and emotional equilibrium, but caused further weakening of my flesh, leading me into many fleshly lusts and temptations. Of course, this was smoothed over and assuaged by performance of Organization instructions. I sought flight from conscience in time counting and time reporting to the Watchtower Society, in bookselling for the Watchtower Society, in religiously attending three to five meetings a week arranged for by the Watchtower Society, in carrying out their instructions. I sought not forgiveness and strength from the throne of God through Christ Jesus.

■ Called to Bethel

Consequently on this fine Thursday afternoon in June, 1937, I once again, as on that fatal day of August 18, 1924, in Magdeburg, Germany, entered into the innermost portals of the Watchtower hell, namely Bethel. As I sat there in the Judge's office, I was afraid. After a few preliminaries, the Judge said, "We want you to come in with us. We need you here. You have the training." Of course, he was referring to my training in the Magdeburg office.

Here it was! Everything in me cried out No, but I found not the strength to utter it. I had unwittingly once again placed myself in the very same position as I had back there in Berlin, when I had been called into the anteroom by the Director of the German Branch of the Watchtower Society and asked to come to help them in Magdeburg. Then, I had walked wholeheartedly into what I thought was Christian service. Now, my heart was not in it. I felt weak. I abhorred the very thought of the slavery I would have to face once I entered into Bethel regimentation.

My inner feelings must have shown on my face. The Judge closely watching me, misinterpreted it. Realizing that I had been good in the field, he naturally concluded that I did not want to leave the field for the confinement of the Bethel Organization. He quickly explained, "Of course, at the time of the next appointments we will make you servant of Companies of New York. And if, after a few months you do not feel you like it here, you can leave." With this hope before me I grasped as a sinking man does at a straw. I accepted. But little did I know that with this acceptance I had opened up an eighteen-year period of torture and torment, from which I barely escaped, in 1954, into the freedom of the sons of God.

■Life at Bethel

Four days after this interview with the Judge, I arrived at Bethel. I soon discovered that things were the same as they had been in Magdeburg. Very obviously the pattern prepared in Germany was used.

At mealtimes the entire family gathered. In the morning the Daily Manna was read, questions were asked about the contents and answers were called for. With only thirty minutes allotted for breakfast, this program made it necessary to hurry if we were going to get enough to eat. The noon meal was interspersed with stories of experiences, and again questions and answers. Nothing in the evening! Everybody was tired, and most members of the family were going to do a lot of talking anyway in some evening meeting.

I noticed though that assembly at the table was not often used to reprimand or scold brethren like it had been in Magdeburg. This was done with more finesse behind the scenes. It seems that they had the thing better organized here. However, from time to time the Judge would bear down on the family at the table. Then it really mattered! The department heads would cringe and twist then! One day he had the purchasing agent on the carpet in the presence of the whole family; and did he make him squirm! It appeared that he had told the purchasing agent to get a fan. It had turned hot, and still no fan! Not only did the Judge make the poor fellow the butt of his scathing sarcasm, but he roundly castigated him before us all.

■ Spies Everywhere

As soon as I had gotten settled in the New York quarters I checked whether they had a spy system. I observed the personnel carefully for a few days, and then approached those brethren I felt to be free of insincerity and duplicity. When I guardedly began to question them as to who the spies were in our midst, they certainly gave me a surprised look. Fear crossed their features, since they thought that I myself might be a spy. I quickly allayed their fears, pointing out that I had already served three and a half years at Magdeburg and thus knew all about the spy system and how it worked. I simply explained that I did not want to do or say anything in the presence of such spies which might get me in trouble. I did not tell them that I also wanted to know them in order to get remarks spread about myself, which would make it easier for me to get released. That first part they could understand and informed me about the men involved.

To my surprise I was placed in the Service Department and given charge of the Pioneer desk. It was a responsible position. It was my duty to handle all assignments, grievances, appointments and services. I had to answer questions and help solve problems. I suppose my long Pioneer experience coupled with office experience and training brought me that assignment.

The Office servant introduced me to the Service Department servant who, he explained, was the last resort. With a straight face the Office servant seriously told me this man knew everything. I had never before seen a man who knew everything, and naturally I looked with keen interest upon him and found a pair of knowing eyes fixed on me and particularly noting my reactions to that remark. When I saw that, I pokered up my face. He was evidently satisfied with what he saw. He purred, "We will get along nicely."

I took to my work easily, and soon mastered my job. Next to me sat a member who I instinctively felt was a reporter for the Office servant. Not being quite sure I tested the status of this member by telling in all confidence that I thought this office system was antiquated. Only a day later I was called to the sanctorum of the Office servant and told that the system used had been evolved over the years and that it suited our particular job. He advised me that since I was new here I should make any suggestion I had to him. Of course, I knew that was good office procedure. But what he did not know was that I was trying to find out who of my neighbors were his spies. Naturally he told me by this conference that the member to whom I had confided was his spy. In one way or another I soon learned that the brother to the right was true blue and no spy. In front of me, on the other hand, was another spy.

It did not take long for me to realize that the setup in New York was just as bad as had been that in Magdeburg. After putting up with it for about two months I had enough of it. I wrote the Judge a note asking him to relieve me, reminding him diplomatically of his promise that I could do so if I did not like it. That did not go over very well. Inasmuch as the Columbus (Ohio) Convention of 1937 was at hand I was asked to stay until after the convention. I was put in charge of transportation and organized a special train.

In the meanwhile it became very clear that I was under surveillance and was even being followed. Often a brother would get to my father's house in Washington Heights ahead of me, to see whether I was actually going home or going somewhere else. I knew from what we had done in Magdeburg, that they were gathering a dossier about me, which they would use to hold me in line were I inclined to break free. I decided I was going to give them a merry ride and really do a lot of things which I knew at some time would come home to roost. The folder of my dossier was filling up! I wondered when they would use it.

To my amazement I was allowed to leave Bethel in apparent good standing after the convention. I was permitted to remain as Unit servant of Manhattan, which position I held from September 1937, until August 1938.

To my complete surprise, in view of my relationship with the Society, when the Theocracy of 1938 was established I received the assignment to become an Exactor, or Zone servant, of Northeastern Ohio and Northwestern Pennsylvania. Upon receiving my assignment I was given specific instructions and also told about the failure of the companies in this area to raise issues. It was explained that this was what clearly was expected of me.

⁎ fifteen ⁎

A SEVEN STEP PROGRAM

▪Use of the Phonograph Is Introduced

It was during the time I am now discussing that the use of the phonograph originated. The Society was beating down the charges that Jehovah's Witnesses were booksellers. They also wanted to refute the charges that they were engaging in a moneymaking scheme—which in reality is the basic purpose of the bookselling devised in 1922.

The answer was found in the use of the phonograph as an "opener" in the door-to-door work. The Judge's speeches on six-minute recordings were already being used on our own transcription machines. These records had also been used by hundreds of radio stations every Sunday. But the Judge's rabid attacks on organized religion, the obnoxious tactics of Jehovah's Witnesses, were prompting responsible people in America to use their influence to get the larger stations to refuse to sell time to Jehovah's Witnesses. More and more stations were dropping out in the metropolitan areas and in the population centers of America. Only the smaller ones in the more sparsely settled areas, that had a hard time to sell their time in any case, continued to sell time to Jehovah's Witnesses. In this manner the radio was becoming increasingly ineffective as a propaganda medium, the more so since it was particularly in the metropolitan areas where the Watchtower Society wanted to build up its prestige and strength. After all, it was now bent upon becoming a mass organization and thus had to work where masses of people lived.

Faced with waning propaganda facilities in the metropolitan centers and with increasing charges of being merely "booksellers," the Society decided to issue a manifesto declaring that because of boycott of the "Message of the Kingdom" by the radio stations, they would now go directly to the people. The money once spent for radio time would henceforth be used for phonographs and recordings.

■Not Given to Generosity

Of course, the statement that the Society was discontinuing its payment of radio broadcasts was misleading. Most local companies of Jehovah's Witnesses paid for their own time. The Society very seldom paid the bill. But it made good reading.

The Society is not designed or inclined to spend money or to give anything free. It is primarily organized to receive and get. It autocratically refuses to render any accounting of income and disbursement to its hundreds of thousands of slaves, while at the same time it forces them to report everything in minutest detail. Of course, it is able, in its characteristic way, to find Scriptural justification for this policy. It piously echoes the words, "Mine river is mine own" (Ezek. 29:3). To this day the leaders maintain and stoutly declare that they have exclusive fishing rights in this river, or channel, as they call it. They certainly will allow no one else to fish for money in it!

When in 1941 I founded the W. J. Schnell Co., with the intent to supply Bible versions and research volumes, I was flatly and firmly ordered by the Service Department in 1944 "to desist from selling books"—for myself, of course. It was entirely agreeable that I continue to sell books for the Society as I had done for the past twenty-two years. I firmly rejected this attempt to curb me in making a living in the only way I had ever learned to do under the Society's own tutelage. In 1951 they finally came out and definitely condemned the methods of my company.

■ Benefits of Censorship

But back to the use of the phonograph. By now ostensibly coming to the home to play recordings by Judge Rutherford "free of charge," because we were being boycotted from doing so on the radio, we had a powerful appeal to people in general. It opened many a door. A witness would play a recording first, discuss it a bit, and then would offer the book along with helps for further information on the topic which the recording had broached. This ruse was effective in getting a hearing for the Judge's message. And it sold books!

Censorship, if handled right, is the best advertising for huge sales. We found that out in the years following the radio station boycott and utilized it to the full. Censorship not only created a wide and intense interest in our books, but it completely whitewashed us of the bookselling charge. It made all arrests, trials and convictions leveled against us as booksellers without a license, appear as rank persecution. It helped foster the idea that all Jehovah's Witnesses were really bona fide ministers of the gospel

(which you know by now to be a far cry from the truth).
Censorship proved to be our friend!

■ Seven-Step Indoctrination Program

After a while an ingenious seven-step course of indoctrination was developed and perfected. These are the seven
steps of brainwashing by which a Watchtower Kingdom
Publisher is fashioned!

The *first step* was the getting of books into the hands of
a person. Any method that achieved that result was
acceptable.

We did not find this unduly difficult due to a number
of circumstances and conditions. We dealt mainly with
people who were professing Christians. We naturally utilized to the full their readiness to buy Bibles and books
pertaining to religion. They regarded their contribution as
a commendable work of charity. Their sympathy for us
was aroused by the fact that we were persecuted and
derided.

The *second step* was the back call. Ostensibly the back call
was made to encourage a purchaser to study the book he
had acquired. A back call record was filed with the company, to insure constant visiting—at least one call a month.
A second purpose of this record was to effect continuity
of effort in behalf of the person visited by always building
upon what had been done before.

The *third step* was to get the person called on to agree to
a weekly study with the Publisher of the book he had purchased. This weekly study was termed a "Home Bible
Study." This was a deceitful misnomer. The course had little to do with the Bible. The text book was a Watchtower
Society published book.

This back call was actually the first direct step of indoctrination. It was used to dislodge any and all of the sub-

ject's loosely held ideas on religion and its practices. Then the book was used to implant new ideas. A person who bought this bill of goods had now become "a person of goodwill" in the jargon of Theocracy. He was gradually loaded up with as many of the Society's books as were in print, and he was inveigled to subscribe to the *Awake* and *Watchtower* magazines. This, so he was told, was our Bible course. If a Kingdom Publisher could be maneuvered into having two or more such book studies a week, he would read the Watchtower books twice or thrice a week. In this way he would slowly become accustomed to phrases used in the book, and store them up for repetition. Gradually, by such repetitious reading with new students Jehovah's Witnesses begin to recite in parrot-like fashion whole portions of the book.

But it was having a second favorable effect. In this *book-selling, back calling, book study* the Society had a highly successful brainwashing scheme for Jehovah's Witnesses and their converts alike. It eliminated insensibly all individual patterns of thinking on any given subject of the Bible, or of religion. It set a new and uniform concept. It is in this manner that the Watchtower Society developed abject *Organization mindedness,* later called *Theocratic mindedness.*

Early in this Home Bible Study course we began to nudge him toward the fourth step.

The *fourth step* was the area book study. For this purpose the city was divided into areas. The meetings were usually held on Friday under direct company arrangement. The study conductor was appointed by the Society and worked in conjunction with the company.

Whereas up to this time the book had been the only source of new light to the "person of goodwill," he now was to learn through the give-and-take of a well regulated dialogue. The purposes of the back call and Home Bible Study were maintained and advanced. Slowly loosely held

Scriptural doctrines and concepts were replaced with Watchtower doctrines.

As Theocratic thinking was being achieved in the study itself, Theocratic doing was gradually presented. First we used events with which all were acquainted to "debunk" the normal outlook of the people in general, and replace it with the fatalistic idea that the world was coming to an early end and would soon be destroyed.

For each season we would have what we called "special debunkers." Around Christmas time we would maintain and dramatically demonstrate that Jesus was born in October; around Easter we would explain that Easter was a pagan holiday and that the egg, the bunny, the pomegranate were merely pagan symbols. So on throughout the year we would have special seasonal "debunkers."

Each week in area study we would dwell on what we had discovered to be the pet peeves of those who attended. First we would enlarge their grievances, and then we would explain to them that in what they were doing they were actually fulfilling the Scripture. We told them that actually the prophet Ezekiel had written about them, and they must be of that class which the prophet Ezekiel predicts in Ezekiel 9, "who sigh and cry for the abominations of the things done in the midst of them."

After these persons of goodwill had been brainwashed enough, they no longer felt one with their former associates, but could only find fault with them. They had now been brought to the point where they were ready to form new associations and to have the Organization line openly fostered among them.

The area book study was conducted on the conference style. It was a give-and-take affair which normally followed a definite routine. A question would be asked about a paragraph and various answers would be given. Others looked up the cited Scripture, and still others finally read the paragraph. This method proved novel and interesting to the "people of goodwill" who had been largely passive in their church affiliations, and they took to this method avidly. Soon they would want to be well read on the subject before meeting time and so would read the lesson and look up the Scriptures in advance. To this they were constantly encouraged in order to make the findings of Scripture passages easy for them. It was necessary for us to make them feel that they were studying the Bible!

The illusion created by looking up Scriptures here and there in the book study successfully obscured the fact that only 6 1/2 percent of the Scriptures, and that in a disconnected way, were used in Watchtower books. Even this 6 1/2 percent was feigned and weighted down with 93 1/2 percent Watchtower verbiage. With this 6 1/2 percent of Bible truth, distorted by 93 1/2 percent Watchtower jargon, the Mark of the Beast was subtly branded onto the forehead of the people of goodwill. That is, slowly they began to think alike, to use the Scriptures alike in the same manner and the same portions. Thus was destroyed the God-intended use of Scriptures as spiritual food prompted by the Holy Spirit in individual application and was created a corral type of mass thinking.

The *fifth step* was to lead the person of goodwill into a wider area of Watchtower indoctrination. This was the attendance of the *Watchtower Study* on Sunday, usually at a Kingdom Hall. The conductor here was usually a servant, flanked by a reader and a questioner. A definite number of paragraphs, usually half of the main article, was the text for consideration on a given Sunday. The questions printed at the bottom of the *Watchtower* page were used.

Here a great fuss was made over these "people of goodwill." They received constant attention, and great effort was made to make them feel at home. It was impressed on them that they were "strangers within the gates," and they were made to feel that they were fulfilling Scriptures by their being there. They were shown that they could soon become one of the mixed multitude, or Jehovah's Witnesses, by preaching to others that which they had learned.

Of course, nothing at all was taught them about Jesus and the way of salvation. They were shown that Armageddon was just around the corner, and that if they stayed within the City of Refuge, which was God's Organization, they would most assuredly find salvation. Notice, how now their thinking had already been changed. The concept of salvation by Christ Jesus had been eradicated from their minds and hearts, and they had been planted body, soul and mind into the Kingdom Hall of Jehovah's Witnesses.

Thus the people of goodwill adopted an entirely new pattern of thinking. The churches, or other organizations from which they had been successfully weaned, were now to them part of Satan's organization, the enemy soon to be destroyed. They themselves, on the other hand, were now basking in God's favor, since they were now in "God's Organization." This Organization became to them like the ark of Noah, which was being built while the destiny of the world hung in the balance. When the great storm of Armageddon would break "the religionists" and the worldly ones would be tragically destroyed; but those associated here would be saved! They were declared safe only as long as they thought and acted in the Society sanctioned way and remained in close contact with the Watchtower Organization.

Thus the brainwashing was well on its way to accomplish its dual purpose, which was (1) to create mass concepts for thinking and living, and (2) to create clannishness and intolerance towards all others in the world, expressed in an attitude of being "inside" and others being on the "outside." This fifth step, thus, was the formal induction into the community concept as preached by the Watchtower Organization.

HOUSE TO HOUSE RECORD

STREET . . . . **TERR. NO.** . . . .

Symbols
  I — Interested
  CA — call again
  BC — back-call

  B — busy
  NH — not home
  V — vacant
  NI — not interested

  B — opposed
  C —child
  M — man
  W — woman

House No.	Apt. No.	Sym-bol	Placements Remarks	House No.	Apt. No.	Sym-bol	Placements Remarks

The worker who calls at your home enters your house number on a form like this one, and records the reception you give him.

Back-Call Follow-Up Report
(To be turned in after each back-call)

Name _____ Terr. No. _____

Address _____
Date back-call made . . . . Literature placed . . . .
( ) Back-Call   Records Run (List numbers) : . . . .
( ) Model Study   . . . .
( ) Book Study
Has this person attended a *Watchtower* study or service meeting? _____
If person not interested, check here ( ) and attach original Back-Call slip.

_____
Name of publisher making call
(Total number of back-calls should also be reported on Publisher's Field Service Report)

S-3

If you show interest, the worker will call back at your home and send a report on this "Back-Call" to his superiors.

PUBLISHER'S FIELD SERVICE REPORT

To be turned in at least once each week. May be used after each day's service if desired.

Name _____ Date _____

Remarks: _____

_____

Total Books	Total Booklets	Hours of Field Service	New WT. and Awake! Subs	Individual Magazines	Back-Calls

8-4   3/49

Printed in U.S.A.

This is a cumulative report of the door-to-door calls which the worker regularly sends in to his home office.

Study Conductor's Report   Month _____ 20 ____

(To be turned in to assistant company servant)

Conductor _____ Publication studied _____

Held at _____ Address _____

Study held on _____ In Terr. No. _____
     (Day of week)   (Hour)

| | ATTENDANCE | | | |
	NEW INTEREST (Those who have not commenced attending headquarters meeting)	ASSOCIATED (Include publishers and inactive)	TOTAL (Not including study conductor)	REMARKS
1ST WEEK				
2ND WEEK				
3RD WEEK				
4TH WEEK				
5TH WEEK				

Show number of different persons attending this study during the month, as follows: New interest . . . . Associated . . . . New interest attending for first time . . . .

On this form the "Study Conductor" makes a report on the success of his efforts

Cleverly thus was the groundwork laid for the *sixth step*. If a person of goodwill really came to believe that he was saved by being *inside* of God's Organization, then, of course, he also believed that all on the *outside* were doomed! It was against this backdrop of urgency that the persons of goodwill were encouraged to go out and help save the lost, especially those in the churches. Again, Scripture was pulled in to serve the Watchtower purpose. The newcomers were told to "go out and do likewise." They were urged to do unto others, what had been done unto them.

But in order to do this right it would be necessary for them to take the *sixth step:* attend service meetings and publish in harmony with Organization instructions. The service meeting, they were told, would train them how to use the proper methods, use the proper books, and to do effective group witnessing. At these service meetings they would be trained how to present the books, how to conduct back calls, how to conduct book studies, and *how to get contributions of money.* Nothing at all was said about prayers, or spiritual living. What was more important was to know how to behave as a Kingdom Publisher, how to make out report slips, how to count time, and how to fulfill the quota. In this sixth step they were to learn to work instinctively according to Organization instructions, and thus receive the Mark of the Beast on their right hand, even as they had received the mark on the forehead in step five. So now they were ready to be initiated into the *Watchtower Mystery Religion* as *Kingdom Publishers* in good standing!

This brings us to the *seventh step*—baptism. As this person of goodwill continued to attend meetings regularly, and as he became a good Publisher, he was told he must now symbolize his consecration in water immersion.

This rite usually takes place at circuit assemblies, or conventions. Since Jehovah's Witnesses deny Christianity in not believing in spiritbegetting and being born again of "water and blood," they use the baptismal rite in its single sense only, the outward sign of official entry into God's Organization, or "city of refuge."

In the light of performance as Kingdom Publisher baptism is the token of leaving behind one's personality and individuality and every personal aspect of the religion of Jesus, and a declaration that the one who receives this rite will henceforth stay under this symbol and sign as a good Kingdom Publisher. Only after they have become regular Publishers and have been publicly inducted into the Organization by water immersion, will the Society actually recognize them as Kingdom Publishers. The Watchtower leaders have strict instructions that no one can be appointed a servant by them in the Organization unless he has been water immersed. Thus now individuality has been buried into the mass or the Theocracy. To be sure, he has lost his soul or individuality. But look, he has gained a whole world, The New World Society status as a Kingdom Publisher!

What benefit does baptism bring him? His departure from "the true faith," they say, will bring him into judgment. His life must remain completely regimented by the Organization until death releases him. All worship, if such it can be called, must be conducted after a standard set by the Society, and calls for monthly time reporting, attendance at meetings, attending area studies, holding home Bible studies, using only the Society's literature, and of faithfully collecting as much money as possible in contributions and turning this over to the account servant.

Gradually this routine becomes the *alter ego* of the Jehovah's Witness and he does automatically and mechanically what he is directed to do. As long as he does this he is in good standing. He is in the city of refuge! He will escape Armageddon!

If he is faithful, several possibilities are open to him. He may be recommended to become a servant in the company, then a Company servant; or he may be awarded the privilege of going to Bethel. He may be declared a Pioneer, thus becoming eligible to go to the Watchtower Bible College with the possibility of becoming a servant of the brethren or a missionary in foreign lands. Once he steps above the common basis of a Kingdom Publisher he has a chance to become a Watchtower prince, or even a Director of the Society. The Watchtower Kingdom Publisher can go no higher than a mere Watchtower prince and that only upon condition he slavishly follows the Watchtower highway of the New World Society. The Christian, on the other hand, is a King and a priest in the Kingdom of God. Which do you choose?

■The Result

Thus during the years from 1935 to 1938, in the dawn of the Theocracy, we worked in New York City and other metropolitan centers to develop this system of things. We had as our goal to capture, brainwash and establish thousands of Kingdom Publishers, making them all think alike, like robots. When in 1938 the Theocracy was decreed, all these fell down in abject submission before this newly erected "Image of the Beast" of the Watchtower religion of "buying and selling" (Rev. 13).

All the companies of Jehovah's Witnesses at that time voted in a resolution declaring that henceforth and always they would accept all instructions and appointments handed down by the Watchtower Society. All shreds of congregational independence were thus given up, together with every semblance of a personal Christian religion. A new world organization based on the concept of robot-like obedience and performance had now been realized and would now expand to become a New World Society. It is described by Jehovah's Witnesses as God's Organization or

Kingdom. It is in actuality nothing more than a dictator-ship of the Faithful and Wise Servant Class in Brooklyn.

Ashamedly I confess here that I had a part in devising and originating such channels of indoctrination during my first tenure in Magdeburg from 1924–1927, and then in America from 1931–1938. Particularly as a Company servant in New York from 1936–1938, I was busy helping Bethelites develop the back call and the book study, the use of the phonograph recording, and finally the very effective seven-step program of developing an organization of human robots.

❖ sixteen ❖

ACTION
IN NEW JERSEY

■ Truly a Slave

I continued to serve the Watchtower Society with my hands and with my mind and heart. I was a slave in the truest sense of the word. I did not want to do what I was doing, knowing clearly how wicked and how wrong it was. I realized that I was helping to raise a Frankenstein, which would surely turn upon me and destroy me. Yet circumstances and surroundings forced me to continue in it.

I now know that I was held enslaved because I failed to study God's word by itself without the distorting *Watchtower* "helps." When in 1943 I finally began to awaken to that fact, I gradually grew in strength and in spirit, to come fully free in 1954, thirty years after I had entered into slavery on August 18, 1924, into Watchtower Bethel of Magdeburg, Germany. But back there while training others for their slave labor and leading them into captivity, I was held in captivity by the very means I used on others—the Watchtower Society published books, booklets and magazines, which alone I read.

Yet through God's grace enough Scriptural truth entered
into my heart and my mind to keep a modicum of individual life active and to preserve my soul from destruction by the vicious brainwashing. But I paid dearly in every
way for this independence, especially in mental torture
and torment. After having done these things in obedience
to Organization instructions, deep remorse would enter
my soul and sadness would fill my mind. But when the
next instruction came along, my feet followed a well
directed path, even into jail, if it had to be, without hesitation—a regular Zombi!

■ On the Boardwalk

Thus it was when I received an assignment to go to
Atlantic City, New Jersey, in the summer of 1938, I went
willingly. I was sent with the express purpose of creating
an issue. The Society wanted the Witnesses to use the
famous Boardwalk as a grandstand during the summer,
during which season millions of people would frequent it.
It appeared that Mayor White had permitted the Salvation Army to use the Boardwalk for their band and to make
collections. That gave us a wonderful opportunity. Without asking for a permit, the Witnesses began to preach
there. They were warned to desist. When they continued,
they were arrested. When they finally did apply, they were
refused a permit upon the ground that their work was different from that of the Salvation Army. The Mayor
explained that the Salvation Army was accepted everywhere as a charitable organization and that not one of the
guests of Atlantic City would therefore take offense at their
appearing on the Boardwalk. Politely the Mayor pointed
out that the same could not be said about Jehovah's Witnesses. After all, they were just emerging from a five-year
campaign throughout New Jersey in which hundreds of

them had been arrested and convicted. The Mayor felt that the appearance of Jehovah's Witnesses would therefore create friction. Thus he turned them down.

The Society now moved in to make an issue of this, the very thing which the Mayor wanted to avoid. It was arranged for the Pennsylvania and New Jersey divisions of Philadelphia and Trenton to use mass action. Plans were made for a daylong witness throughout Atlantic City, to be culminated by a meeting held in defiance of the Mayor's edict, at a specially designated place on the Boardwalk. Pamphlets were printed, announcing the time and place of this meeting, and the reason why it was being held. I was selected to be the "patsy," or fall guy, to give the talk.

Upon receiving this assignment I felt like I was really on the spot. I underwent all sorts of troublous thoughts. But I had been arrested many times before in the Watchtower cause, about sixteen times to be exact, both in Germany and in the United States. I had faced mobs before, too, and had been stoned twice and one time practically brained with a heavy oak chair. So, while I did not like the prospect, I felt that this was the price I had to pay.

■To Jail We Go

Promptly at 7 P.M. on the designated Sunday, I ascended a table on the Boardwalk and began to speak as advertised. A huge crowd of about 25,000 had gathered, few of whom could hear me. I had spoken about ten words, when two plainclothesmen stepped up and asked me to step down, saying, "You are under arrest." In order to accentuate and make the most of the disturbance I added a few of my own moves. I had told the Publishers to use my arrest as a signal for them to go through the crowd and leave pamphlets with the people giving them the Watchtower version of the reason for the arrest. They carried out this instruction faithfully, and seventeen were arrested. Many of those arrested were women and children. Thus I had created a real splash!

While waiting for the "black Maria" to arrive, we were quite a public spectacle! That was exactly what we wanted. It was excellent advertising. As a Christian I was truly ashamed that Sunday night, for being arrested as a common violator of the law of a city in the midst of which I was a stranger. I knew all the time that I was not being arrested for preaching the gospel as we claimed!

I was taken to jail and fingerprinted. Soon two reporters appeared, representing the two daily papers of Atlantic City, and I was allowed to talk with them. I told them that I had expressly come from New York City as a representative of the Watchtower Society to defy Mayor White. It seems that the Mayor at this time was out of favor with the press. So, of course, our story made good reading. Needless to say the whole thing raged big headlines in the next day's papers, calling attention to the arrest and its purpose. I had created an issue which was to go on until finally, in another case, we obtained a permanent injunction against Atlantic City, and thus could assemble unmolested on the Boardwalk.

■ Troublous Thoughts

Alone with my thoughts, lying on the upper bunk in the cell, I could not find sleep that night. For one thing, the place was filthy, crawling with vermin. But worse than the filth in the cell, was the filth I felt crammed into my mind and heart. Here I was, supposedly a Christian, picking a fight like any common political agitator with people I had never seen, and against whom I had absolutely no grievance. This was quite unlike my Lord, of whom it was prophetically said, "He never raised His voice in the streets." I had ostensibly come here to use the Boardwalk for preaching; yet that really was not the purpose at all. It was merely to go through the motions of a defiance for an ulterior purpose! I was miserable, and felt that I was the worst kind of creature.

When in the morning we were allowed to leave the cells for breakfast, other inmates began to talk to me. One vagrant, who had been picked up drunk the night before, approached me and asked, "What are you in for, buddy?" I replied, "For preaching the gospel." At that he looked me up and down with utter contempt, and unbelievingly with a frown on his face said, "They would hardly do that," and walked away. In his face and in his behavior, I could see that he thought I was a liar. In my heart I knew he was right. I knew that I had not come to preach the gospel but to create an issue for my Theocratic masters!

▪Rewarded

I was welcomed back to Brooklyn as a hero. The Atlantic City affair put me in solid with the Society, and assured them, so they thought, that I would follow through in the field. Thus they assigned me a choice chunk of the Theocracy of 1938, the territory of Northeastern Ohio and Northwestern Pennsylvania.

When I was given my assignment and Zone book I was also thoroughly briefed. First of all I eliminated the cliques that ruled and troubled the largest company of Jehovah's Witnesses in my Zone. Next, the Witnesses in this area had failed to raise a single issue, backing down every time they had a chance to do so. I was to raise several issues here for Ohio, and push them through to the Supreme Court. Now I began to understand why I had been tested in Atlantic City. The Society now was sure I would follow through.

One of the Bethelites put it into words when he said, "You are tough enough to do it."

Thus in accepting the Zone assignment, I once again was to become a hatchet man for the Watchtower Society. I was to cause trouble for myself, out of which I would not be able to extricate myself for sixteen years. In the years immediately ahead Witnesses on whose toes I had stepped were to take a frightful vengeance of me, a revenge which I justly deserved.

seventeen

THE THEOCRACY OF 1938

■ The Judge's Dreams

In the sixth chapter I reported on Judge Rutherford's dream in the prison of Atlanta, Georgia, and on his voiced determination to get back at Christendom by evolving a permanent block against it. Well, the Theocracy of 1938 was the culmination of that dream! In introducing it the Judge, in accordance with his usual procedure, quite naturally used the Scriptures as feigned words to trap unwary victims. In this particular instance he quoted from Isaiah 60:17: "For brass I will bring gold, and for iron I will bring silver, and for wood brass, and for stones iron: I will also make thy officers peace, and thine exactors righteousness."

The Judge forgot the Word of God has a two-edged application. If wrongly applied, as now done by the Watchtower Society, the Word of God becomes a boomerang, cutting in another way from what is intended. I firmly believe this to be inherent in the situation conjured by the Watchtower Society.

The Judge sensed that the argumentation for the erection of the Theocracy, as they called it, had to be given more solid semblance of the truth than the mere quotation of Isaiah 60:17 could lend it. So the Judge described Solomon's program for the building of the temple and the city and other buildings, as the blueprint for the Theocracy.

In using this picture in the columns of the *Watchtower*, he gave away the Society's blueprint for the Organization from 1919 to 1938. The Society started out by using Israel's borrowing technique, or spoils collection technique as a pattern for their Advertising Campaign of 1922 to sell books for a money consideration. The Society continued to use step-by-step the history of Israel up to the monachy of Solomon. The giving of the law and Israel's defection in the worship of the golden calf, they aver was exprienced from 1919 to 1931, during which time the overwhelming components of the Mordecai-Naomi class defected. This, of course, had made room for the Ruth-Esther class, in the same manner as the Exodus generation of Israelites died off in the forty years of desert wandering, and was replaced by a new generation which under Joshua was permitted to enter into the promised land. This new generation, the Ruth-Esther class, while still in the desert, had piled up a big heap of books, millions of which had been sold to the peoples of the world. As stones were used miraculously to commemorate the parting of the waters of the Jordan in which Joshua and the Israelites crossed dry shod into Canaan, so this vast pile of books sold between 1919 and to 1931 gave visual evidence of enabling the Ruth-Esther class under the leadership of the anti-typical Joshua to see they had entered into the land of praise, or into Watchtower led Kingdom service. Then, so they claimed, with the advent of 1931 came the reward of this twelve-year campaign in the giving of the name "Jehovah's Witnesses." The assumption of the name ipso facto, also gave expression to their claim to the land of praise, for in very fact they had become the possession of God, or as they put it, "God's Organization."

▪ The Third Tier

During these years of occupation, from 1931 to 1938, Judge Rutherford had taken the lead. But since there was blood on his hands, to use the simile of the condition which prevented David from building the temple, it was now up to a newly constituted Society eventually to build the temple and the city and the buildings of this Theocracy. These men were also mindful of what happened to the Monarchy on Solomon's death. They therefore moved to improve on history by eschewing the leadership of one man for the third layer of the Watchtower Society. The first tier had been under the dictatorship of Charles T. Russell, 1879 to 1916; the second tier of the society was under the dictatorship of Judge Rutherford, 1919–1942; the third tier was now in the making.

They were now creating a committee or *consortium* of seven to take over, to be selected from out of the ranks of the charter members of those who now formed the Society. These charter members were to be appointed by the Society, and these in turn furnished the leaders for the society. Six to eight such charter members were selected from each State of the Union, insuring that Americans would always be in control. From among these charter members were selected the Board of Directors; from the Board of Directors were selected the President, Vice President and Secretary and Treasurer, who in turn filled by appointment vacancies arising amidst the charter members. This was to be the *modus operandi* of the third layer of the Watchtower Society, and in this they hoped to improve on the Solomon Monarchy.

The pattern having been decided upon, the establishment of the Theocracy and the carrying out of the building program was now at hand. The building method for the expansion was a concentrated training program consisting of the seven steps discussed in a former chapter. The seven-step program created the vicious circle of causing all to think alike and work alike. But the two-edged sword which they misused did what it could be expected to do. It cut them off from normalcy, and from the personal religion of Jesus. It meant for them all the end of liberty, and a condemnation into slavery to the New World Society. We can see their end from the beginning. "If any man is for captivity, into captivity he goeth" (Rev. 13:10). Leading millions of Christians into slavery, the Watchtower Society itself has become and is destined increasingly to become a slave to its routine, and thus to lead also itself into captivity.

I once again accepted an assignment in this horrible thing: And I was given some very distasteful tasks to perform. The truth of Revelation 13:10 was also being demonstrated in my life. I had led many into captivity in my life. My record shows that I baptized four hundred sixty-three into the Organization. Now I was but a pawn myself. I was caught in a web of my own weaving.

To start off, I was assigned as cochairman of the Cleveland outlet of the London Worldwide assembly. This was held in the Arena in Cleveland, where we drew 17,000 people. The highlights of this Convention, which was connected by wireless from the main Convention in London, were two talks by the Judge on "Face the Facts" and "Fill the Earth." Both were really policy declarations of the new Theocracy. They were intended to give the Watchtower interpretation on the political events transpiring in Europe at the time, and also to lay a feigned Scriptural groundwork for stopping thousands of young people within the movement from doing what comes naturally, namely, getting married.

■ "Face the Facts"

Of course, Fascism and freedom was a topic of keen interest to all. Fascism was rampant in Europe and war loomed on the horizon. Realizing that the doctrinaire separateness of Jehovah's Witnesses was going to lead them to claim exemption as ministers and conscientious objectors, the Judge declared that the Theocracy was in favor of freedom, and against regimentation. Yet, while the Judge thus publicly made this declaration, we knew that freedom would in no wise be tolerated within the ranks.

In this manner the Judge was creating a background which would prevent any move to declare the Watchtower Society as being opposed to war. He redeclared the Society's neutrality in all war matters. This talk, "Face the Facts," which later was published in a booklet which was distributed by the millions, was the first of a series of declarations which culminated in 1941 in the booklet entitled *Neutrality.* This series of declarations helped Jehovah's Witnesses to stay out of the military service in this country, and earned them only five-year jail sentences where they failed. Its success mightily advanced the Society cause. Even today hundreds of thousands are joining to stay out of possible war activity. This is without a doubt one of the underlying causes for the Society's phenomenal rise and increase in the postwar years.

■ "Fill the Earth"

But while the Judge declared opposition to totalitarianism and neutrality to the outside world, he sounded the tocsin for the start of a relentless campaign to make all

Jehovah's Witnesses absolutely totalitarian. With the advent of the Theocracy came the primary task of training all those coming under its spell. In this training work, here in America and later throughout the world, thousands of young people were preferred, because they had no dependents and encumbrances, and the Society wished to keep as many unattached as possible. For that reason, the new Watchtower Society proclaimed the doctrine "Fill the Earth."

Creating an atmosphere of urgency in the first talk "Face the Facts," with the vista of war ahead, perhaps Armageddon! and as the Judge alluded, using the old Watchtower scarecrow, perhaps the end of the world!! it was easy for the Judge to impress these young people not to marry before Armageddon, since it was so close. Was it not much better to wait until the Millennium to raise their families? Rather stay single now and devote your years to the Theocracy! Later in 1940 this was followed up doctrinally in the book *Children* with the stirring and touching story of John and Eunice. Here were two young Jehovah's Witnesses deeply in love with each other. But, both being Theocratic minded, they decided to wait until after Armageddon before getting married. They decided this because the end of the world was at hand. The Watchtower Society hoped to delay their getting married at least until they got their increase and training program in the whole world well under way.

That they merely used the doctrine "Fill the Earth" as a ruse can be seen from what happened later when the missionary work in foreign lands had been successfully launched. A veritable March of the Millions a la Noah's ark, two by two, then began to the platforms of the Kingdom Halls to be married. This was led by the highest officials of the Society, the hard core of the Theocratic bachelors, who suddenly decided not to wait until after Armageddon, but to get married now, to fill the earth. The charming story of John and Eunice in the book *Children,* so beautifully written, was soon forgotten and that book cannot be procured anywhere now from Jehovah's Witnesses. It has become one of their many organizational skeletons rattling in their secret places.

Like the prediction of the end of the world in 1924, and in 1925, and then the prediction of Armageddon after the war, "Fill the Earth" had served its purpose of steaming up the Witnesses, and is now discarded. That is routine procedure in the Society.

✣ eighteen ✣

BRINGING ZONE I
INTO LINE

Now back to the Zone work! I was assigned as Zone servant to Zone No. 1, State of Ohio.

■ Divisions, Cliques and Jealousy

The first visit to Youngstown disclosed that the Society had gauged the condition of the Company correctly. One group, disfellowshipped some time before, had been reluctantly reinstated. The group now in the saddle consisted mostly of unspiritual Jonadabs. These were trying to oust the spiritual Remnant, which consisted in this case of the younger Ruth-Esther class. In the middle was an unaffiliated group.

Each of these groups saw to it that its spokesmen got to me with its side of the story, each reporting on the other. Being there to spy on them, I naturally listened attentively and formed my own opinions. I did not do a thing there my first trip around, but just let matters ride.

My next Company was Niles, where the same conditions existed on a smaller scale. The territory of this particular Company extended all the way into Ashtabula county, but it was clamoring for more territory. Youngstown held territory almost all over Mahoning county at the time and deep into Trumbull county. It seemed as if all these companies were jealous of their own honor. They all felt they had too little territory, though they already spent most of their time travelling long distance in this territory, making very few calls every Sunday, covering the vast territories they held not more than once a year, and sometimes once every two years.

It was my responsibility to get the Publishers to concentrate on their home base, to organize and intensify their work there, and to follow the procedure of the seven steps of brainwashing and training. In Niles I split the Company four ways, making four small companies out of it, and instructed each of these to forget about all the territory between and to concentrate on their immediate neighborhoods. Of course, this soon forced the old Company servant and his helpers out and new Jonadabs were put in their places.

In Warren there were also three cliques. So little did they trust one another that no one was allowed to give me lodging and board. Instead, they rented a hotel room for me during my first stay, and jointly paid for it. I eventually broke that Company up into three units. By the time I got to Jefferson I had quite a number of people in an uproar.

■ An Ultimatum

The Judge thought that the proper time had arrived to give me a taste of my dossier. So I was awakened at 11 o'clock one night by the Company servant and assistant Company servant of the Youngstown Company. They brought me from Youngstown a letter mailed to me there from the Judge. It consisted of twenty-two typewritten pages in which the Judge really laid me out. To it I was commanded to give a Yes or No answer. Was I going to cooperate, or not? By throwing this dossier at me, they were making sure I was going to perform according to their wishes. I knew when they started gathering it, which was after I had left Bethel, that that is how it would be used.

It did not shock me at all. This certainly surprised my visitors. I could see astonishment written on their faces. They probably had been told I might explode. So incredulous must the report of my behavior have seemed to their superiors in the Adams Street Office, that they sent another Zone servant and a confidant of one of the Bethel cliques to see me the next week in Conneaut, where I was serving that Company. After observing how I conducted the meeting and otherwise checking on me, they were satisfied that I was carrying no grudge.

What they did not realize was, that as a trained servant from Germany of the Magdeburg office, I had long before been trained never to be shocked by anything that Watchtower Society politics might bring forth, but always to carry on unthinkingly and in robot fashion. I was performing here like an old timer, and these boys in Brooklyn were new at this Theocratic dictatorship business. I had only one goal, and that was to make this Zone Theocratic; and nobody was going to stop me!

■The Spy System Extended

This surveillance committee so closely after the Judge's epistle served to alert me. I sensed that the old Society leadership under the Judge was waning and the budding new leadership, preparing to take over after the Judge died, considered this spy system in the field a matter of necessity. In order to work in consortium and by compromise, everyone had to be mediocre. Brilliance or independence were not permissible. It had to be nipped in the bud wherever it showed itself. That is why they considered the spy system necessary to survival.

But even before this, the policy of the Watchtower Society had always been to create classes and to pit one against the other, to create strains and stresses causing turmoil and strife. That is why I liken this organization to the idol Moloch. Within it there is kept going a constant fire, and into this fire are thrown the Kingdom Publishers to be tortured and tormented into submission. I could not get out, even though I could see the handwriting of doom on the wall as far as my position was concerned, with this new clique coming into power. I was in a veritable hell. My thoughts troubled me. My conscience tortured me. I tried to get out, but every time I almost made it something seemed to pull me right back into the caldron again.

At any rate, I must have been given a clean bill of health by the Bethel confidant who visited me at Conneaut. This Theocratic spy told me, "I like what you are doing. Just keep your nose clean."

So I continued to go through the motions.

▪I Am a Faithful Slave

With the dawning of the year 1939 I was set to make the necessary changes of personnel in the Zone. I went to work in true Watchtower fashion. I took all men whom I believed would acquiesce, together with those whom I wanted out of Youngstown, and gave them a pep talk. I told them they were needed to establish the Theocracy in these smaller and newer Companies roundabout Youngstown which I had just organized.

During my second visit to Youngstown, I organized new Companies in Salem, Canfield, Lowellville and Hubbard.

In this way I stopped the Publishers effectively from running all over the landscape, and forced them to concentrate on their own neighborhoods. This greatly increased the effectiveness of the training program. Next I manned the new positions in all these newer and smaller Companies with such brethren whose influence I wanted to break in their own Congregations. By spring of 1939 I had completed one phase of my work. I had broken up everything and recast it into new forms.

I soon learned that I was not liked very much for what I had done. The smarter knew why I had done this. It appeared for a while that open revolt might break out against me. Efforts began to be made to blacken me with the Society. This pleased the new forming leadership of the coming third Watchtower Society very much. It would furnish them the opportunity, when my usefulness was at an end, to use pressure from below to remove me.

■ Creating an Issue

Of course, all this did not stop my work. I proceeded in abject slavery to the Society to carry out the second part of my assignment, to create an issue.

Having organized a new Company in Hubbard, Ohio, I realized that in the village there had always been opposition to our work in one form or another. So, I persuaded the Company there, which had always met in a private home, to rent a hall in Hubbard as a Kingdom Hall. Once that was accomplished, I began advertising the meetings. For that purpose I got a hundred brethren to come into Hubbard from nearby Youngstown. They paraded up and down the streets of Hubbard, with sandwich signs around them, carrying the provocative message, "Religion Is a Snare and a Racket." We were baiting that normally peaceful village in proper Watchtower fashion and it did not take long for Hubbard to react by arresting our people. At first our members were let go on their own recognizance and a meeting was arranged by our lawyers between the Mayor and myself. The Mayor was eager to get out of this, and asked me only to stop for a while parading around the streets with those abominable signs. I refused. My lawyer also was disgusted with me, but I could not do otherwise. I had my instructions. The next Saturday we again appeared in force, and of course, the village of Hubbard acted and arrested about twenty-two of us.

This was my golden opportunity—the opening for the creation of an issue! I moved in fast. The arrests occurred Saturday afternoon, and I called for a protest meeting for Sunday 3 P.M. at the Hubbard Hall, calling in the whole Zone. During the night I hurriedly prepared a pamphlet entitled, *Two Christians Arrested in Hubbard, Ohio,* and a brother who owned a printery printed them for us during the night.

On Sunday morning we distributed these pamphlets to the people and called for a special meeting at our Kingdom Hall. Of course, a huge crowd appeared. When I started to talk the Chief of Police came into the hall and took away our loudspeaker. I then went outside, stood on top of a car and continued my talk. The mob was getting ugly and was beginning to pelt me with rotten tomatoes and all kinds of vegetables. I was prepared for this. I had wisely organized a flying squad to protect things, and this determined phalanx-like group around the hall held the mob at bay. It is really a horrible thing to face a raging mob; but I could not back down. Twice before in my life I had faced this kind of thing. Finally my knees buckled under me and I had to retreat into the Hall and wait for the Police to liberate me.

After all was over, Monday came, and with it the trial. Two were tried and convicted. A fine of $25.00 and costs was imposed. We naturally appealed the case.

The Judge was highly elated over what I was doing and so was the legal desk. The Judge said he especially liked my attitude of fighting to the last ditch and that everything I did in this campaign was O.K. with him. He assured me that I had his full backing and offered me all the money I needed. That did not go over so well with the men in the Adams Street crowd who were grooming themselves for the third tier of the Watchtower Society, and who actually did become the official leaders when the Judge died. But there was nothing they could do.

■Rough Stuff

At the Convention of 1939 in New York City I had further occasion to bring myself unintentionally to the Judge's attention. On one of the last days of the assembly, held in Madison Square Garden, during the main talk by Judge Rutherford to a crowded-out Garden, there was a riot and an attempt to break up this meeting. We had been warned beforehand and long before the Assembly convened some of us were selected and put in charge of flying squads. I had fifteen men in my squad. Each of us was armed with a sturdy walking cane. I was assigned one of the rear balcony sections looking down upon the platform.

As soon as the Garden filled, we observed a large group of people streaming into the rear balcony. My section filled within minutes. I noticed that all of these people carried paper bags which seemed filled with something, I knew not what. As I deliberately brushed against a woman the bag fell from her hand and burst open, revealing that it held overripe tomatoes. Of course, we could do nothing as yet, since no overt act had been committed. But we were alerted from that instant on. No sooner did the Judge begin to speak than those carrying the paper bags began throwing vegetables at the platform below, while others stamped their feet, and yelled loudly. Without a moment's hesitation we waded into that crowd with canes swinging. Our section was cleared in seven minutes flat! I broke my cane in two over somebody's skull, and then used my fists. My shirt sleeves were torn off and I had a few bruises. The talk went on after only a few minutes of pandemonium.

■ Commended and Warned

As a result of my riot-breaking activity I rated a special invitation from the Judge to come to his office. The Adams Street clique did not like that either. The Judge commended me on my riot-breaking, as well as my Hubbard work. It was obvious that I was in favor again with the Judge and he was giving me an opportunity to ask him to take me back into Bethel. That I did not do. After a rather long pause, which was intended to give me an opportunity to voice that request, he looked upon a long dossier which lay in front of him on the desk, and very evidently furnished him by the Adams Street group. There was that dossier again! Very solemnly and seriously he said that someone had written that I was conducting myself improperly toward the girls in the various companies and asked me whether that was true. I was astonished, and of course replied that there was no truth in the report. All the while I knew that the Judge did not believe the charge himself.

Our session being concluded, the Judge invited me to walk with him from Columbia Heights to Henry Street, where all Zone servants were to meet with him at a Kingdom Hall of a Brooklyn unit. During the course of this informal meeting he made me the butt of his sarcasm without mentioning my name, by saying, "And when you get to the companies don't do what one of you is doing, lining up all the girls and then kissing them. That is no way to make Publishers out of them." Of course, everybody roared. The fact that he was "laughing me off" meant that sooner or later I was to be given the proverbial backseat and eventually dropped altogether. The patter I knew all too well. All this was to come as I learned later when once my Zone work was completed. And when it came it came with a vengeance—with persecution and vilification the like I had not dreamed possible. But by the Lord's grace I was given strength to bear all this until I finally broke through to the freedom which is to be found only in Christ Jesus. But an account of that will have to wait.

Much history was still to intervene. That is why many contradictory things will not appear in this account. The Judge and the legal desk were still functioning as leaders. But it was a losing battle. The new clique of the third Society now forming in Adams Street was steadily gaining ground and was getting ready to take over and start their worldwide building program.

Like it or not, I was tied to the waning group in the Watchtower Theocracy galaxy. When I cut myself loose from the Bethel assignment of 1937, which the Adams Street clique had arranged for me, they knew as one of them had put it: "You don't like us here." Naturally that meant that I was to take a backseat sooner or later. Subconsciously I must have been working toward that end myself. I worked myself into such a cul-de-sac by events to follow, that I would eventually be trapped and halted.

▪ Victory at Hubbard

In order to face the issue in Hubbard, we started out again on Saturday's parading with the sandwich signs. Not only were many arrested, but some were beaten, one by the police. Mobs pelted our people with vegetables. This was exactly as we wanted it, and we did not want to end it prematurely. Finally, during the week preceding the third Saturday, I had our lawyer ask the Court of Common Pleas in Warren, Ohio, for a temporary injunction pending trial for a permanent injunction. It was granted, of course.

That Saturday we had no trouble and we really were elated. The trial took place the next Monday and the Judge refused us a permanent injunction, decreeing a cooling off period first. No journal entry was agreed upon. It was left open. In that way the Judge did not put the responsibility on the village officials. But I was determined to force the issue. I telegraphed to the Judge in Brooklyn a request and received permission to call a special protest meeting of Zones 1 and 2 in Youngstown for the next Saturday and Sunday. These Zones consisted of the Akron, Cleveland and Youngstown areas.

Mob violence raged all day long in Hubbard, as thousands of Witnesses flocked into Hubbard and Youngstown. This was the first showdown in the Middle West of the sanguine warfare type they had read about our having in New Jersey. Of course, everybody wanted to be in on it. On Sunday we packed the East High School, the auditorium, the grounds and even the streets. It was a huge success from a publicity angle, for the story carried all over Ohio. It was equally successful from a financial angle, for it gave me enough funds in the legal fund really to put up a good fight. The resolution adopted by this protest gathering had been written by the Judge himself. "And now," so the Judge put it, "you have carte blanche." This meant you can do anything you want.

I realized we had to get at Hubbard in another way, through their pocket books. Thus we decided on a two-pronged attack aimed at bringing in a permanent injunction at the end of the cooling off period. First we rented seven plots of land facing as many different highways leading into Hubbard from all sides. On them, as close as possible to the roads, we had huge signs erected and stretched out, bearing the message— HUBBARD, OHIO, IS UNFAIR— HUBBARD, OHIO, IS UN-AMERICAN! These stations were manned for twelve hours each day with Publishers from the various companies of the Zone. From these stations we distributed booklets and provocative pamphlets. You might say we laid siege to Hubbard, and much violence took place. As my second move I had thirty-two of our people who had been arrested file civil damage suits for false arrest. I had the brother who was beaten by the police file a separate suit. The picketing kept up all the while that this move developed.

The first suit to come up was the one against the police chief. It was clearly evident that he had used brutality, and our strategy was to get a jury trial. We insisted that we wanted trial by jury in all of the cases. I instructed our lawyer routinely to exempt all Catholics from jury service, and make a show of it. This made the Protestants who were selected feel like they had to uphold religious issues (at least, so I hoped).

Things looked bad for Hubbard, and our lawyers were jubilant. As the trial progressed, I sprung new instructions to the lawyers—which they did not like! I asked for a recess, and a conference with the Judge and the village officials. We convinced Hubbard that they might be made to pay through the nose unless . . . I pointed out that we were not after money, but wanted a permanent injunction. It worked. We got it! As our end of the bargain, we dropped all damage suits. Hubbard had been brought low as we had intended and the next day picketing stopped.

The Judge asked me to write an account of the entire case. It later appeared in the magazine *Consolation*. But many of the brethren really had it in for me now. To my surprise they actually had wanted to collect money from Hubbard out of this. When I was faced with this realization, I was amazed! You live and learn.

With the victory of getting a permanent injunction in Hubbard ours, I set out to train Publishers throughout the Zone in the seven steps, and to build the Companies along Theocratic lines. We had many flat salute cases, and started our own private school for children expelled for refusing to salute the flag. I really kept things stirred up all the time. The local people were not a bit pleased with this and I did not blame them. But they had voted away their rights of independence to the Society, and they were to learn that from now on they were never to be rid of the Society's "eyes and ears" within their midst. They were now to be made Theocratic subjects, bowing to the Theocracy of 1938. It was fellows like me who were assigned to put that across!

■Martin vs. Struthers

The legal desk kept after me to raise an issue and bring it all the way up to the Supreme Court of the United States. I selected the town of Struthers, Ohio, for this purpose. For years Youngstown witnesses had backed down in Struthers, where officials refused to let the witnesses work on Sunday, because they had a "bell ringing ordinance" to safeguard peace on Sunday. Their claim was that our doorbell ringing on Sunday mornings would awaken them from their slumbers prematurely. When I read the ordinance it conjured up wonderful opportunities in my mind. I mused, If the Struthers people do not like doorbell ringing by us on Sunday mornings, how come they stand for the ringing of church bells on that same day?

As a result of my musing I set a campaign for a given Sunday morning. As it progressed, the Mayor soon accosted me. Being a kind man he suggested we leave peaceably and ordered that the ones who had been arrested should be released. But this time we did not back down. We came back for more the next Sunday. Arrests occurred and I called for help from Youngstown; but the leaders there refused to budge. They had the backing of the Adams Street clique of would-be leaders of the Society, while I had instructions from the legal desk. Besides, I had charge of the Zone. So I turned around and called in the Zone and the issue was joined until the jails were filled. I knew that when you start a fight, you cannot stop to think whether it is right or wrong. You just slug or fight until you win or lose.

In the subsequent trial those who had been arrested were convicted. We chose to appeal one case. This case became known as the *Martin vs. Struthers* case, and as such stands in the journal entry in the Supreme Court of the United States. We carried this case all the way up to the Supreme Court, and the "bell ringing ordinance" was knocked out. So ridiculous was the Struthers contention about being awakened Sundays by our bell ringing, that one of the Supreme Court Justices in questioning the attorney for Struthers asked, "What do you do when the church bells ring?" It left the solicitor hanging in mid-air, for he dared not speak disparagingly about that!

But the Adams Street clique was now in the ascendancy in proportion as the Judge's health was going from bad to worse. Brooklyn was not applauding me this time! I received a letter instructing me to retard my accelerated visits and to get down to a weekly routine of visits in rotation. I knew now, as it was brought to my attention, that I was about to be replaced because of Struthers; but the legal desk intervened in my behalf for reasons of its own.

■The Society Safeguards Its Interests

With World War II looming ahead, the Watchtower Society was mindful of the authoritative status of their

Zone servants. Fearing that some, following their early training, might make unguarded remarks regarding America's war effort, and recalling what had happened to the Society in 1917 and 1918, the Society decided to terminate the Zone work as of November 30, 1941. Uncannily they accomplished this just about a week before Pearl Harbor brought us into a shooting war.

The Society now assumed the position of absolute neutrality. While they had contended and taught that they were taking care of God's work in the Theocracy, they now switched front and put each one of us on our own. It mattered not to them whether that meant jail, concentration camps, or what might transpire. They would not be responsible, they said, and they washed their hands of all responsibility for us. It suddenly suited their purpose to remember Galatians 6:5, "Let every man bear his own burden." They changed their Theocratic tune that they were the Beast of Burden carrying our burdens. Leaving the Witnesses in the lurch and to shift for themselves as best they could, the Society now proclaimed neutrality in order to keep its organization intact to fight another day. In many lands including Canada, the Watchtower Society was banned. But Brooklyn was astute enough to stay in operation at all odds. For, they really were working feverishly for their next step, namely, "WORLD THEOCRACY"!

I have tried to give you a picture of the workings of the Organization in these formative years of the Theocracy of 1938, particularly of the behind the scenes fight for power and position between the newly forming Adams Street clique and the old guard. I have told you of their use of spies, flunkies, stooges and dossiers. I want you to know and see that the Watchtower Society was like any other organization bent for power. Their claim to preach the gospel of the Kingdom, while sincerely believed by many, was actually made to cover up the real purpose for forming so powerful a religious organization. Today it claims

America as its background, tomorrow it will claim the world, and it hopes to give tone and direction to the world society of nations for a thousand years to come. In anticipation of that total victory it already calls itself "THE NEW WORLD SOCIETY"!

✦ nineteen ✦

ESTABLISHING A WORLDWIDE THEOCRACY

■No Escape

On December 1, 1941, with my zone assignment honorably terminated, I was free. Or was I? I thought I could escape by requesting an assignment in Florida, but my request to be assigned in Florida was denied. Instead I was assigned to become a part of the very Youngstown Company which I had decimated and which had risen up in opposition during the Struthers arrests. I was to be a special Publisher in nearby Campbell, which belonged to Youngstown, strengthening the group there to become a Company. My assignment as Zone servant having come to an end, I had the status of Pioneer under the full direction of the Adams Street office, wherein the new clique now reigned supreme. In pinning me down in Youngstown they were going to give me the choice of taking a backseat and buckling down or—get out!

▪ A Losing Battle

So I started out to Pioneer again. And before my opponents in Youngstown could act, I stole a march on them. I visited all Jehovah's Witnesses in Campbell and sold them on the idea of forming a Company, and without delay effected its organization. The Society and Youngstown were not a bit pleased, but there was nothing they could do about it, as I was acting according to my written instructions. In thus escaping the direct jurisdiction of the Youngstown Company, I thought I would be able to hold them at bay, or arm's length so to speak.

I now began to build the Campbell Company. But it became almost impossible for me to do any good. Youngstown, working under cover, saw to that. They were determined to prevent the emergence of a truly independent Company in Campbell. They continued to make back calls in Campbell and used this opportunity to work against me. They visited book studies and asked the Publishers to come to Youngstown. Most of these Publishers were of foreign extractions, since Campbell itself is almost all Slovak, and they were afraid. The Youngstown group played on that fear to my disadvantage. Thus I never really got the cooperation of the Publishers in Campbell. While I placed many books there I had to make money in other ways to pay my expenses. Besides, I did not succeed in getting many new Publishers into the field. It appeared that I had been played to a stalemate.

In the meanwhile World War II had begun, and I also became the object of other forces outside the Organization. Complaints were launched against me with the FBI. It seems that I was accused of being un-American (possibly because I lived long years in Germany) and as a chronic troublemaker. Thus I was under surveillance by both the FBI and the Youngstown Company employed by the Watchtower Society. I was now getting it from both sides.

Those were trying times for me. The stress and strain became so great that I was eventually to suffer a breakdown.

▪ The "Clean Organization" Reorganizes

But, let us go back to the Watchtower Society and its doings. Having publicly, like Pilate, washed their hands of all responsibility for what might happen to any of us individual Jehovah's Witnesses, the Society enshrouded itself in a cloak of neutrality. Then it piously referred to itself as a "Clean Organization," thus attempting to whitewash itself of its obnoxious acts and misdeeds of years gone by. This they accomplished by making an about-face. How was that done? The path was rather devious, but we will try to follow them.

The Society was still using Israel and its Monarchy as its pattern for action. Judge Rutherford and the Old Society had been likened unto David and his military organization. This suited the rising Watchtower regime admirably. Because David had "blood on his hands" he had not been permitted to build the Temple. So also the Theocracy of 1938 could therefore not be built by the Judge and the old Society. It had to be built by the newly constituted Society, which represented Solomon.

There was one rub. Solomon had finally defected and become unfaithful. If the new regime were to use the Scriptural pattern, how were they to escape these implications? That was easy. The Society would be reorganized so that it would no longer be controlled by one man. A consortium of leaders, the Board of Directors, which under both Russell and Rutherford had been but a rubber stamp affair, was now to assume the actual leadership. In this way the Society hoped to make better provision for its perpetuation and effect greater stability in leadership.

In order to provide even greater assurance of continuity the new leadership decided to form a New York corporation to supplement the Pennsylvania corporation. The Society had been incorporated in Pennsylvania as a benevolent organization dependent upon voluntary contributions. But now Jehovah's Witnesses had been legalized by court action as a religion of "buying and selling." The new charter under which it was incorporated as the Watchtower Bible and Tract Society, Inc., of New York State, declared and established that fact for all times to come.

In planning the reorganization, the leaders decided upon a definite number of charter members, six to eight from each of our forty-eight states, all appointed by the Board of Directors of the Society. In this way the Board created its own source of power. Furthermore, since the charter members are subject to dismissal by the Board, this body has assured itself of being perpetuated in power.

In thus reorganizing itself the Society sought to ensure that there never would be a recurrence of such scenes as had been occasioned by the death of Charles Russell and the emergence of Judge Rutherford. But in order to achieve permanency as an Organization the Watchtower Society had done that which it had always vociferously condemned. It had, using its own terminology, compromised with the world, or with what they contemptuously termed Egypt. In other words, they had gone to the State of New York for help, rather than to trust in the Lord to perpetuate the Organization.

By incorporating in such a manner that its charter members were perpetually to be picked from the forty-eight States of the United States the Watchtower Society assured itself of an American character. This indicated the Society's decision to expand into the world with an American label. It is difficult to overestimate the astuteness and wisdom of that decision. For, with the war won, America's military prestige and financial power became unmatched in the free world. The possession of an American passport was an open sesame in all countries of the West and in their colonies, as well as in all neutralist countries of the world. No sooner had the war ended, than the Society began its missionary work and campaign in all the world, and under the American label it rode the crest of the popularity and prestige and power of postwar America. That is the basic reason why, coupled with expert training of her missionaries and perfect organization of her work, she succeeded so phenomenally. Only in countries behind the Iron Curtain has the Watchtower Society fared ill because of her American label. But then she shrugs her Theocratic shoulders and says, "You can't have everything." Well, she can wait there.

There you have a picture of that fine "Clean Organization"—a bright shining Theocracy, streamlined and sleek. It had done all in its power to create a halo of godliness around its head. But that halo is quite transparent. To all who have eyes to see the Watchtower Society stands visible as an organization which employs the same principle of expediency which guides all political and commercial organizations. In adopting this policy, the Watchtower Society betrays the fact that it is actually an integral part of this present world order. In using the half truth and subversion according to patterns laid by the world it gives a concrete denial of its claim to godliness.

■The Theocratic Ministry Course

Assuming Solomon's toga, the new Watchtower Society was dedicated to the building and educational program. The educational program was almost forced upon them. The Society's program of indoctrination by which she had brainwashed Jehovah's Witnesses had always had a negative purpose. It had been designed to eradicate former concepts and to annihilate individual thinking, and to replace these with static Watchtower concepts and Theocratic mindedness. This Theocratic mindedness proved satisfactory when employed within the narrow confines of the Theocracy, or in house-to-house work or proselytizing. However, glaring inadequacies showed up when Jehovah's Witnesses were pitted against educated men in Christendom, men who knew their Bible and had a comprehensive understanding of the truth.

This was clearly demonstrated when young Jehovah's Witnesses appeared before examination boards to defend their claims of being ministers or conscientious objectors to escape military service. The ignorance of the Jehovah's Witnesses was truly appalling. Once in Cleveland one of the members of the examination board remarked, "You claim to be a Minister and you can't even find Deuteronomy?" which for a fact this young man could not find. But such occurrences multiplied by the thousands, alerted the Society and they decided to eliminate this condition. Because of this lack, the Theocratic Ministry Course was born. We generally associate the ministry with Scripture and preaching of the Word. Therefore, we might logically expect the Ministry Course to have something to do with Bible truth. Such, however, is not the case. It is instead a systematic course of advanced training in Theocratic truth, and the uses of the various forms of argumentation. An hour a week was set aside for this "Ministry" Course, and to this day it is a definite part of the curriculum of the weekly Service meeting. To conduct this course mature brethren were appointed school servants.

■The Gilead Bible College

In the middle thirties the Society had purchased a large farm in upstate South Lansing, New York, in order to meet their own food requirements. The Society ran a large dairy farm also. The farm was a highly successful enterprise.

But the production of cheese and baloney was not the only value of that farm. In the early forties the fear of war was rife. For this reason the Society decided to build a large building on the site of the farm. First of all they planned to use this building as headquarters if Bethel in Brooklyn should be bombed out in the impending war. Second, it was to be used as a Bible College to train missionaries for foreign work when that became feasible.

When it became evident that the war would not touch our shores and thus incapacitate Bethel in Brooklyn, the Society decided to go ahead with the building of the Watchtower College, which it named the Gilead Bible College. Mature Jehovah's Witnesses, all full-time servants, were called in, and the first six-month course began at Gilead. Those graduating received a diploma. Many were sent into small towns to build up Companies, others were appointed servants to the brethren, which service had taken the place of the Zone servant or exactors.

■Missionary Work

All the graduates were actually biding the time when visas for foreign countries could be obtained. After all, the Society was setting its sights on becoming a "New World Society." Since the war was still raging in Asia and Europe, the Society concentrated largely on South and Central America. That is why the first classes of the College included Spanish in the curriculum.

The missionaries in the foreign fields used the same methods as we employed in the American section of the Theocracy. They first sought to establish a nucleus, however small. Next, they concentrated on the "buying and selling" routine. Then slowly they introduced the "seven-step" brainwashing indoctrination program. In this manner the work began to expand into the world, and the Society moved toward the goal of becoming the world religion.

▪Missionary Motives

Jesus left these parting instructions to His church, "Go ye therefore into all the world, and make disciples of all nations, baptizing them into the name of the Father, and of the Son, and of the Holy Spirit; teaching them to observe all things whatsoever I have commanded you; and lo, I am with you always" (Matt. 28:19–20). The Watchtower already in 1922 had set out to "preach the Gospel of the Kingdom." But they did not do so to disciple the nations, that is, to bring them to Christ as brethren, or equals before the throne of grace. No, they did so to gain money to make the Organization strong and powerful, and to gain prestige for the Organization. With "feigned words" they "made merchandise" of men. After 1931 they developed the scheme of unspiritual Jonadabs, so that they could gather a vast multitude of "hewers of wood and carriers of water," slaves of the Theocracy. Their motive, thus, for going out into all the world is not to baptize them unto Jesus Christ but to initiate them into the Theocracy; not to teach them all things whatsoever Jesus Christ commanded His disciples to do, but to force them as slaves to perform Watchtower service; to put grievous burdens upon these who are already heavy laden, and thus to enslave them two-fold (Matt. 23:15).

There is now the third tier of the Watchtower, or the third phase of the Watchtower Society. The first phase was under the dictatorship of Russell, from 1879–1916, with a "wound unto death" between 1916 to 1919; then the second Watchtower Society from 1919 to 1942 under the dictatorship of Judge Rutherford under whose tenure the Society became

The Faithful and Wise Servant Class; and finally the third and present Watchtower Society, from 1942 to 2942, so they hope, for a thousand years, a New World Society, a class Society ruled dictatorially by a consortium of self-perpetuating Directors. In the building and erection of this huge edifice, or the Theocracy of 1938, the Watchtower Society hopes by the practice of its religion of "buying out time out of individual lives for their purposes and making them report that time spent to them" and of selling books, booklets and magazines for them and bringing in the contributions, to draw millions into its slavery, cracking its Theocratic whip over their hapless backs, as generations come and generations go, for the next thousand years.

Will they succeed?

twenty

WHO IS THE
BIG BAD WOLF?

The desire for fair play, brotherly love, yes, love for my enemies, engendered in my heart as a result of the teachings of Jesus Christ, often came into conflict with the hateful, vindictive and rabid attacks of the Watchtower publications sold by Jehovah's Witnesses: attacks upon the clergy, upon religion, upon Protestantism and Catholicism.

■I Was Puzzled

These very attacks, their minuteness, and the persistency with which they were carried out may have contributed much to wise me up to the purpose behind them. Not only did the Society's blatant attacks on the clergy, religion, and most all other organizations except our own, jar my Christian sense of right and wrong; they gave rise to a growing desire to look behind the scenes for the reasons for them.

Naturally, so I argued with myself, if we attack something as being basically evil and wrong, then, it must be diametrically opposed to what we ourselves practice and do. And, as I looked behind the scene, I was amazed at a comparison of what the clergy, religion, Protestants and Catholics do, with what we ourselves were doing. Why, we were all doing essentially the same things! Only in many instances, we were doing them much more effectively, and being new at it, with much more zeal. That was a startling discovery! If, as Jehovah's Witnesses, we were being led to believe by the books published by the Watchtower Society, the things the clergy, religion, Protestantism and Catholicism were doing were evil, then why were we doing the same things? And why, in doing them were we doing them under cover, while attacking these so-called enemies?

Even if the clergy and religion and Protestantism and Catholicism were our enemies, so I reasoned, then as Christians we were not handling them right. We certainly were not doing as Paul suggests in Romans 12:18–20: "If it be possible, as much as lieth in you, live peaceably with all men. Dearly beloved, avenge not yourselves, but rather give place unto wrath for it is written, Vengeance is mine, I will repay, saith the Lord. Therefore, if thine enemy hunger, feed him; if he thirst, give him to drink; for in so doing thou shalt heap coals of fire on his head."

In my youth I was taught that basically man has only one enemy, Satan. But as I became more and more involved in the Watchtower Religion, I noticed that the Society through its various books was furnishing myself and Jehovah's Witnesses, with an ever increasing list of enemies. As a member of the Organization I nodded my head and goose-stepped right along. But within I had moments of concern and pangs of conscience.

■ "Religion Is the Instrument of the Devil"

Among the many enemies of the Society, the book *Enemies* lists religion. In fact, the entire third chapter is devoted to a deriding of religion. In order indelibly to establish religion in our minds as an enemy, the Society states without any hesitation, "Let this be remembered and kept in mind henceforth: Religion has ever been the chief instrument employed by the Devil to reproach the name of Almighty God and turn the people away from the Most High" (page 66, paragraph 1). That is a pretty strong statement, is it not? But there is more to come.

See whether you can follow this one. "The Devil is the great enemy or adversary of God, and his religion therefore is an enemy of the Almighty God. The Devil is man's worst enemy, and his religion is likewise a deadly enemy to man. The Devil's Organization is symbolized by an unchaste and impure woman, which is called 'Babylon.' Therefore all religions are of Babylon, and particularly the leading religion known in the lands of 'Christendom'" (page 71, paragraph 1).

Note here the typical Watchtower approach. An incontrovertible historical fact is mentioned and the conclusion which it wants to make is associated with this fact. In this particular instance they first state the divinely ascertained truth that Satan is the enemy; they next associate him with "Babylon," and then associate all religion as the devil's religion by calling it "Babylon." Having thus injected the devil, then Babylon, as his religion, they use a modicum of Scripture to give seeming plausibility to their conclusion.

Then they go on and quote from Scripture (on page 71, paragraph 2), "It is therefore written in the Bible concerning Babylon that 'she has made all the nations drunk with the wine of her fornication'" (Rev. 14:8). And from Revelation 17:5 comes then, so they aver, the clincher to this argument, "And upon her forehead was a name written, MYSTERY, BABYLON THE GREAT, THE MOTHER OF HARLOTS AND ABOMINATIONS OF THE EARTH." So now they had religion and Babylon identified. It naturally followed that all the Scriptural statements of condemnation of Babylon now applied to religion. Of course, it is a bit difficult to see the logic. But it is enough to enable the Watchtower Society to make the dramatic summarizing statement: "All of which shows that Religion is the instrument of the Devil employed to oppose, to defy, to mock and to reproach the Almighty God, whose name is Jehovah" (page 71, paragraph 2). In further support of this conclusion, this paragraph cites the sixth chapter of the book *Prophecy*, published by the Watchtower Society in 1929, which chapter is entitled, "Satan's Organization," of which it there shows that religion is a part.

As we continue our perusal of this revealing publication, on page 118, under the subheading "Murderers," paragraph 1, we come across this startling accusation: "All liars and murderers are religionists. Whenever a murderer is about to be executed, he has some religious practitioner to say some senseless words over him, which is supposed to save him, but which does no good. The Devil was the originator of Religion, and the Devil is the father of lies and 'a murderer from the beginning' and ever thereafter" (John 8:44).

What conclusions were Jehovah's Witnesses intended to draw from the above? The end of the chapter furnishes it: "There is no such thing in existence as 'the Christian Religion,' because all Religion proceeds from God's enemy, the Devil. 'Christian Religion' is a misnomer, fraudulent and deceptive . . . (page 130, paragraph 1).

Having thus declared all religion as an enemy and a fraud, there remained but one more step. That was to brand the practicing of religion a racket, and those organizing it, racketeers. A whole chapter in the book *Enemies* (chapter V) is devoted to "Racketeers." Later a whole book devoted to *Religion* and bearing that title was published by the Watchtower Society in 1940. There the Society really rams epithets on its archenemy. "Religion is a snare and a racket" (page 104), "a snare to entrap" (page 30, 1; 31, 1; 52, 1; 53, 2), "the besetting sin" (44, 1), "demon worship" (83, 2). "Devils and demons use it" (44, 1; 78, 1), and it was originated by the Devil (18, 1; 104, 1).

You may ask, How can a sane person go along with these accusations? I can only answer, as I have done before, that as a Jehovah's Witness I moved along in what I now see as a hypnotic state, befuddled and confused by the constant flow of Watchtower jargon.

■The Roman Catholics, too

The Roman Catholics come in for some scathing accusations. The entire chapter "Racketeers," in the book entitled *Enemies,* from pages 142–193, after defining Racketeers, sets about to declare the Catholic religion as a racket. After once more stating that "Religion labeled 'The Christian Religion' is a racket invented by the Devil" (page 146), it states, "And in time Pagan Rome blossomed into what is known as Papal Rome, which from then, till now, practices what is called 'The Christian Religion, . . .')page 148, paragraph 1). Beginning here the author follows through with blow upon blow. He shows how "fear was used," (page 154) and then "Pretense" (page 155); how the Hierarchal form of Theocracy was used over the "population," and how false teachings and inconsistency were employed (page 159); how organization methods were designed to increase numbers and wealth (page 170), and how Purgatory became the doctrine for collecting money to create organization wealth (pages 171–179); how ceremonies created formal worship (pages 181–185) and how images began to be used as means of "organized worship" (pages

186–191); and how they have "houses" all over the earth within which is practiced deceit (page 192, paragraph 2).

As I read this dissertation, when first published, I stood aghast to realize by comparison how the second Watchtower Society, from 1919 to 1942, was built up by means of the very practices for which it condemned the Catholic Church as Racketeers. I know you will be struck by the same similarity. It is almost as if they have used as their blueprint this list of accusations of the Roman Catholics.

Let us take a look at a few of the parallels. Jehovah's Witnesses under the guidance of the Watchtower Society, have constantly utilized *fear* of the end of the world and Armageddon as a club to keep Jehovah's Witnesses in line, and it has scared many folk into their Theocracy. You will recall how they used *pretense* in the early years when they declared that 1925 would bring an end to the work and world, in order to promulgate a new slant on doctrines, how they misused the Scriptures to buttress their claim of being God's Organization; and how they created their role as The Faithful and Wise Servant Class, setting up the very *hierarchal form* which they condemn in the Catholics. Then you will remember how they began to use the very *principle of organization* of which they accused Christendom, *in order to gain numbers and wealth,* the very things they accuse the Catholic Church of being after. You will recall how they instituted the "Advertise, Advertise, Advertise the King and the Kingdom" Campaign of 1922 in order to sell books and collect money, at the same time that they accused the Catholics of using the doctrine of Purgatory to gain money contributions for the Organization. Instead of the *formal worship* of the Catholics and meetings, and in the place of images which they accuse the Catholics of using, they have standardized a worship of buying and selling (Rev. 13:10), with charts, quotas, and other business paraphernalia. Then we have seen how that once their religion of "buying and selling" was legalized by the United States Supreme Court and the Courts of the land, they began to build "houses" (or Kingdom Halls) all over the earth, to practice their religion of buying and selling—the very thing they accused the Catholic Church of doing (chapter on "Racketeers," in *Enemies*). Is it not striking how closely they follow the practices which they condemn in others? By their own judgment they shall be judged!

You can now well imagine that when I read these accusations of religion, Catholicism, and Protestantism, there welled up in my heart and mind the soulfelt query, "Who now is the Racketeer?"

▪ Protestantism Is "the Offspring of the Great Harlot"

Still another matter is the Watchtower attack on Protestantism. This jarred me even more than did the attack on religion and Catholicism, because it hit closer to home. From the early sixteenth century my family were of the Protestant faith, and a number of them died in the Thirty Year War. Members of my mother's family stem from Huguenot stock. Protestantism is an ingrained quantity in my life.

As early as in 1926, in the book *Deliverance*, the Watchtower Society called Protestantism "the offspring of the great Harlot" (page 270, 2). In the book *Religion*, it speaks of Protestantism as "following devilish wisdom" (page 82, 1, 2). In *Enemies* they state that "Protestantism plays into the hands of the Hierarchy" (page 225, 1, 2). In the book *Riches*, published in 1936, they call "Protestantism now part of the 'great whore'" (page 285, 1). In *Vindication*, Vol. III, published in 1932, they make bold to assert that "Protestantism is more reprehensible than Catholicism" (pages 203, 1; 305, 1; 306, 1).

I could go on quoting multifarious pages and paragraphs, from the voluminous writings published by the
Watchtower Society, but that would only be a repetition
of the type and caliber of pronouncements made by "The
Faithful and Wise Servant Class."

∎The Clergy Are "Children of the Devil"

The Jehovah's Witnesses are known for their attacks on
the clergy. From whence this hatred of clergymen by Judge
Rutherford and the Watchtower Society? As you recall from
earlier chapters, the United States Government banned the
Watchtower Society during the war years, 1918–19, dissolved the Society, and imprisoned Judge Rutherford and
others. Upon being freed from Atlanta, the Judge began his
violent opposition to "organized Christianity" and the clergy,
using his arrest as basis for hatred. Instead of following the
Christian principle of winning over those who had ill used
him (if that is what they actually had done), he proceeded
to oppose and attack them without mercy.

Why am I so confident that this hatred of the clergy
emanated from the grudge held by the Judge and the Society for causing their work to be closed down? In the book
Religion, published by the Watchtower Society in 1940, we
read on page 225, paragraph 2:

> In 1918, because Jehovah's people were restrained of lib-
> erty and service the religionists, and particularly the high
> clergy-men, were much at ease, and so Jehovah says con-
> cerning that situation: 'And I am very sore displeased with
> the heathen (the religionists, who claim to serve God but
> who do not) that are at ease; for I was but a little displeased
> (with my consecrated people in 1917 and 1918), and they
> (the religionists) helped forward the affliction (upon my
> faithful servants).' (Zechariah 1:15.) Thus the religionists
> did by heaping reproach upon God's consecrated people,

claiming them to be enemies of God and calling them by all manner of false names and shamefully treating them.

Zechariah would be quite amazed at those interpolations in the parentheses. And I am sure that God is not honored by this misuse of His Word.

Watchtower Society promulgated thinking was arbitrarily injected here, to describe the crucial period of the eclipse of the Watchtower Society during 1918 and 1919 as a punishment meted out to Bible Students for omissions on their part. Inferentially this was placing the blame for this "punishment" upon the Bible Students' failure to acquiesce abjectly to Judge Rutherford's assuming the presidency of the Society and to the formation of a new Watchtower Society under his leadership. But this failure on the part of the Bible Students was less reprehensible, so the above quotation alludes, because it is taken for granted that they would have come around sooner or later, and accepted the new leadership of this new Watchtower Society. In order to cover up the inaccuracy of this assumption, as is evidenced by the subsequent need for purging 75 percent of all Bible Students between the years 1919 to 1931 for failure to come around to Watchtower leadership, a scapegoat had to be found. And, what class was more convenient than the clergy! As the quotation from the book *Religion* shows, in misusing the Zechariah Scripture "they helped forward the affliction." In this far-fetched manner, Watchtower thinking was channeled into hatred for the clergy, and served as an effective smokescreen over the extended purges of Bible Students in the years of 1919 to 1931.

This diversionary attack against the clergy was carried on in every book published from the book *Deliverance* on. In this particular book the clergy are labeled "allies of the Devil" (page 264, 5). Without any hesitation or qualification they are accused of being "emissaries of Satan" (page 35, 1) and are said to "teach and advocate war" (page 229, 1).

In the book *Government,* published by the Watchtower Society in 1928 the following accusations are leveled at the clergy: "they aid profiteers" (page 16, 2), "make sport of true Christians" (page 269, 1), "they prove themselves as children of the Devil" (pages 100, 1; 101, 2).

I do not wish to weary you by an enumeration of these invectives, insinuations, and accusations. But you should hear a few from the book *Prophecy,* published by the Watchtower Society in 1929. The clergy are charged with being "guilty of blood" (page 282, 3, to 284, 2; 285, 3; 293, 2). They "make God a liar" (page 23, 1), are "Satan's mouthpieces" (page 205, 2 to 206, 1), and "thieves against God" (page 239, 4 to 241, 1).

These accusations could be multiplied manyfold. But let this suffice to illustrate the persistent and unrestrained bombardment of the clergy.

▪ Which Is the Commendable Spirit?

As I once more go through some of the Watchtower Society published books, I stand amazed and aghast at the versatility of abuse heaped upon the clergy, leveled against them as a class, and in contrast the complete absence of retaliatory measures on the part of the clergy, when so often they had good grounds to be effective. In fact, as early as the year 1935 there began to grow in my heart and mind a smoldering suspicion, that the Watchtower Society and their Faithful and Wise Servant Class amidst loud declarations and avowals of having replaced the clergy as leaders of Christianity, were much less Christian in their pronouncements and behavior than were the clergy whom they denounced. As this sort of evidence mounted, during my active years as a Theocratic exactor, I became less and less sure of the Watchtower's claim as having been "given all the goods"—as they put it.

I know that many of my former brethren, as they read the attacks against the clergy which I quote from Watchtower books, and as they note the absence of retaliatory measures by the clergy, they too will be amazed at what such a new look will unearth! Such a detached look at the whole situation will quickly free Jehovah's Witnesses from the mass hypnosis of Watchtower thinking, and will bring a new evaluation. Love, the language of God, and of Jesus Christ, of the apostles and of Christianity, cannot express itself in such a sterile atmosphere of book placing, time counting and quota performing. Love works through the heart and mind of the individual.

There is no doubt that it was the advertising campaign begun in 1922 with books which gradually but increasingly caused difficulties. A clear, calm, and objective analysis of the books saturated with attacks on all concepts of beliefs held by people everywhere, would at once show the true culprit, or villain in the act. But in order to prevent Jehovah's Witnesses from discovering the culprit, the Watchtower used the clergy as their "whipping boy." If the clergy were actually as wicked and powerful as the Watchtower Society in its books avers, then reflection would at once cause one to marvel why they did not eliminate the Watchtower Society. They certainly had innumerable openings! But in books like *Preservation*, by directing its attack on the clergy the Society prevented the accusing finger to be turned upon itself by Jehovah's Witnesses who lingered in jails, paid fines, were mobbed, ostracized. I hope many of my brethren will think upon that.

■ "Fear God, Honor the King"

The religion of Jesus has always had high regard for law and order. Allegiance to God and one's own nation are an essential part of the spiritual makeup of Christianity. To be sure, true allegiance to God comes first; but you will recall that Jesus actually wept over Jerusalem and her lot. He did not in a bitter spirit of revenge and with evident relish condemn her to Armageddon. Paul said, "Let every soul be subject unto the higher powers. For there is no power but of God: the powers that be are ordained of God" (Rom. 13:1). Peter admonished us to "Fear God. Honor the King" (1 Peter 2:17). To condemn therefore all governments as of the devil, as do the Jehovah's Witnesses, negates effectively the practice of Christianity in its rightful sense. In their negative attitude toward government, Jehovah's Witnesses have been led to lose wonderful opportunities to honor God. Since I do not take delight in casting unfavorable reflections upon anyone, I will refrain from quoting from Watchtower books which have engendered such a negative attitude. But they are there to read for all who care to examine them.

■No Longer Puzzled

When, upon reflection and upon taking a new look at all Watchtower published books, I began to see—really see—how the Watchtower religion worked, it was as if all the organization-engendered scales fell from my eyes. I began to see the enormity of the slavery into which I had fallen. But to see it, and to get free from it, are two different things. In the following chapter I will describe what it took to get actually free.

✛ twenty-one ✛

COMING OUT OF THE LABYRINTH OF WATCHTOWER SLAVERY

■ **Prayer for Delivery**

The fact that I have come out of abject Watchtower slavery to freedom is sure evidence of the grace of God. Inasmuch as I was deeply enslaved for thirty years and then escaped from this prison house which I myself helped build, certainly argues that nothing is impossible with God. It testifies to the thousands now enslaved by the Watchtower Society, that they too can find a way out. In fact, it points the way.

I had long known that the Lord expected of me devotion to Him rather than slavery to a human organization. But I am a weak man, and the Society knew this full well. It knew my background. It knew all my weaknesses and all my fears. It had a record of all the mistakes I had made. They knew how to scare me and how to play on phobias they had engendered in my makeup during the long time they held total sway over me. And I knew that they knew it.

If I have the courage to write this book, and put it out publicly, knowing full well what it means to my future safety and my ability to make a living, to my possessions and my life, it is solely because I am under a vow to do so and God is giving me strength and sustaining me. One night when I was in sore affliction of mind and spirit, I prayed all night long for the Lord to remove the very bad situation in which I found myself. I promised God that if He delivered me, I would do what I could see was His will—expose publicly the slavery I had been in. I can testify that from that night on I have been freed from the scourge that controlled me for so many years. Thus it is in fulfillment of this vow that I write this book, trusting in the Lord who is always faithful, to protect me.

■Supplementing My Income

When in December of 1941 my work as Zone servant came to an end, and I began Pioneer work at Campbell, I had to find some way to supplement the income I derived from selling Watchtower books, booklets and magazines. As Zone servant I had been clothed, fed and housed by the Zone.

Since I had extensive acquaintance with Bibles and books, I decided to go into the book business for myself rather than sell only books issued by the Watchtower Society. So I established the W. J. Schnell Co. Knowing from experience the appalling lack of knowledge among Jehovah's Witnesses, I felt that I could furnish them with books which would broaden their outlook. In this way I could make an honorable living at the same time that I rendered a much needed service. By splitting my profits with Jehovah's Witnesses I helped them secure the various versions of the

Bible much cheaper than they could have gotten them elsewhere. In fact, the Society itself carried many of these same versions and books in its price lists and, of course, charged the full price, or all that the market could bear.

I was able to handle this book business from my home by mail and from 1941 to 1943 I did but a small business. Then I received a letter from the Service Department of the Society directing me to desist from selling these books, since they might interfere with Theocratic knowledge. What they meant, and what they should have said, was that they wanted to have to themselves the whole field to make money on these books and they wanted to have complete control over what books Jehovah's Witnesses bought and read. Of course, I rejected their order to terminate my private book sales. You may be sure that in this way I did not endear myself to the powers that be. But when I pointed out to them that I used this business to earn money to defray my expenses as a Pioneer they had no answer.

▪Life Can Be Miserable

During these years I really had hard sledding in Youngstown. Every step I took was watched. People came to my office ostensibly to buy books, but they never bought. Actually they just came to spy on me and I knew it. Life was pretty miserable. With malicious intent to destroy and break up my business, they spread, among other gossip and vilification, the rumor that I was using my Watchtower connections to make myself rich. At Campbell things were virtually at a standstill. I was just barely able to keep a Company going there. Things dragged along like this until 1949, when I finally got tired of it all— tired of the constant surveillance and worn down by persistent opposition and ill will. So I left the special Pioneer service to which I had been assigned. This meant either that I would have to be transferred to some other spot, or I would have to stay and function as an ordinary Pioneer.

Ironically, while first I wanted to leave here and they would not allow me to do so, they now wanted me to leave, and I did not want to. No doubt the reason for their change of mind was the fact that I had succeeded in establishing my independence. Well, it was also the reason I had changed my mind.

In 1946 I hit upon the idea of publishing an interesting, informative sheet which I called *Book News*. It featured different Bible versions and books, describing them and explaining their value. This news sheet soon caught on and my mailing list skyrocketed to about three thousand names, almost all of them Jehovah's Witnesses. My book business, handled by mail right here from my home, flourished beyond expectations. I next instituted a system of sending on approval two books a year to every regular recipient of the free *Book News* and thus got my business total to grow. In the meanwhile 1949 had come to an end and with it the Campbell Company. I stayed to serve as Pioneer.

By this time my mind was beginning to awaken from the hypnosis of Watchtower corybantism. I had been reading a lot of material throughout the years from 1941 on. In particular I had been reading the Bible by itself, without Watchtower Society helps. By God's grace the Holy Spirit entered my being and began to work powerfully upon me. Spiritual strength returned and I became more outspoken for truth other than that published in the *Watchtower* magazine—although I did not oppose the Watchtower. My change of mind and attitude was no doubt noticeable in my *Book News* and by 1951 there were repercussions.

On February 15, 1951, I received a letter from the Society informing me that I was being taken off the Pioneer list because I was no longer fulfilling my time quota and because I was publishing the *Book News,* and was sending books on consignment to Jehovah's Witnesses. The Society obviously felt that they alone had the right to sell books, and send books on consignment. They felt that the prerogative of teaching was theirs alone. They judged that "buying and selling" Watchtower books, and reporting time and sending in the contributions to them was a religious practice and that I as Jehovah's Witness had no right to use these practices of worship by "buying and selling" non-Watchtower books for my own expenses. So they fired me as Pioneer. They told me I could come back, as soon as I stopped doing what I was, and began "buying and selling" (Rev. 13:17) their way.

I probably was the first person to infringe on this Watchtower business from inside of the Organization. Those from the outside who infringed on this worship of "buying and selling" were uniformly attacked and defeated.

My full-time service, of which I had been so proud, consisted of twenty-one eventful years of full time service. During all this time I had faithfully made the required reports to the Society. I had certainly bought out a lot of time for the Society's use from out of my individual life. In the years of my blindness I bowed to the Society's every wish. I fought for her at the risk of my safety and life. This record, according to my superiors, was to be my evidence that I was saved and could not be destroyed in Armageddon. Well, it was now wiped out in one night! Nothing ever happened to me that hit home so deeply, and at the same time was so illuminating as to the deplorable condition in which I now found myself. I felt as one left standing in a barren wilderness. I realized with shock that all these years I had been building upon sand. Now the storms had come, and my religious edifice had come crashing down. There I stood. My mind was a blank. My heart was a spiritual void. I had nothing left to worship with or in. Once, I had built as a Christian on a true rock, namely

Christ Jesus. But . . . that was long ago. Would I ever be able to get back to that happy time?

The props were naturally knocked from under my book business. I experienced what amounted to almost a complete boycott, as all my customers who were Jehovah's Witnesses left me. I was deeply in debt, having made large commitments because of a growing business. If I had been indebted to Jehovah's Witnesses solely, I would surely have been forced into bankruptcy. They, after all, had no mercy on me. But fortunately the businessmen with whom I dealt in the book world understood what had happened after I explained it to them. They took pity on me and allowed me to work things out for myself. Since then, by the Lord's grace I have paid up this large commitment. I can assure you that the payment was made as difficult for me as Jehovah's Witnesses knew how.

So weak, perplexed and floundering was I at that time that I did give in to the extent that I discontinued publishing my *Book News*. I foolishly thought that in this way I might stave off the boycott. But if I thought surveillance and boycott would cease when I in this way backed down partially, I was sorely mistaken. My telephone would ring as often as six times a day—and when I answered there would be a deathly silence at the other end. I received numerous anonymous letters telling of all the things that could happen to me if I continued. I was visited by spies under the cloak of being brethren. This was followed not only by threats but by vilification and character assassination with a view to impairing my credit. Mentally I was disturbed. Spiritually I was at sea. Physically I suffered a heart attack.

■Full Surrender

Gradually I began to regain my spiritual balance as I read God's Word without the heady Watchtower wine. The more I learned of God's purposes in Jesus Christ, the more clearly did I see that I must speak out, and that I must publish a warning and expose this horrible monster which had grown up in the past seventy years to threaten Christendom with destruction! I could see and I felt the latent urge of the Holy Spirit prompting me to do so.

But do not get the idea that the battle had been won. Alas, I was a coward. I had already tasted what these former brethren of mine could do to me. And, having done this sort of thing to others, I could always sense what they were about and what they would do to me. Besides, it seems that as you develop a capacity to torment and torture others, as I had done for thirty years, at that very same time you lay yourself open to feel more deeply and keenly torture and torment inflicted upon you. I had to learn that through experience, and it felt like hell's fire! At one stage I succumbed, and tried to drown out the insistent promptings of the Holy Spirit by the use of strong drink, which, of course, eventually worsened my lot immeasurably. This affliction was abetted by some of my enemies, who saw to it that funds were available to me for this destructive purpose.

Oh, how afraid I was! The ones assigned by the Society to watch me sensed what was going on, and they continued to raise new fears, new phobias, and cast more aspersions. They certainly had ample and fertile soil. For all these years I had failed to be true to myself as a Christian and had lived according to a double standard. As a result my judgment had become warped, and I had repeatedly made wrong decisions and many, many mistakes.

Having been cared for all my life in all my needs by buying and selling books for the Watchtower Society, and having imbibed their perverted ideas about money, I was ill prepared to handle money properly. This contributed to my dilemma. Being unable to repay my debts at the time, my conscience plagued me, and these people knew it, and played on it. Subtly and maliciously they pointed out how the rug could be pulled from under me. You have no idea how this kind of thing can be used to wear a person down. Rapidly becoming a drunkard, physically and mentally sick, filled with fears and phobias, I was in a straightened condition which was leading me straight to death.

Then one night, I could stand it no longer. I was home alone that night, my wife being away on a visit to her parents. I sank to my knees. I threw myself unreservedly upon the Lord. All night long I poured out a confession of all the wrongs I had done as a Watchtower slave. And now as I look over what I have written in this story of my slavery I am startled to realize that it was precisely this that I told the Lord that night. This story is only a retelling of that confession to God. I poured out an account of all my sins, iniquities and failures before the Lord that night. But I also thanked the Lord that in spite of it all He had not forsaken me. I thanked Him for preservation and for all the wonderful things that He had done for me while I was thus doing these wrongs.

Finally, early in the morning, I promised the Lord and vowed to Him that I would write an exposé and publish all these facts if He would liberate me of my drinking affliction, and of my fear of Jehovah's Witnesses and the dire things they threatened to do to me.

▪ Complete Delivery

Now as early dawn broke in the East, I arose from my knees. God had heard my prayers. I stood up by the grace of God a free man! I stood up calm, assured, with peace in my mind and heart. I stood up knowing I should never again be afflicted by fear of the Watchtower Society, and Jehovah's Witnesses and what they could do to me, and free of the terrible drink habit. God had forgiven me, and for the first time in thirty years I actually experienced a peace which goes beyond human understanding.

All this happened in April, 1952, and now as I am finally finishing this book it is September, 1971. The wonderful thing about it is that in all these years I have never had a craving or desire for strong drink. It vanished along with my fears, that morning in April, 1952. How do I explain it? It is the Lord's doing in answer to my prayer. It is wonderful!

Delivered from my dual affliction, fear of the Watchtower monster and drunkenness, I began my "walk in the Spirit." I set about my task early in 1952 and have worked painstakingly ever since. The spies were under the impression that they were cowering me as of old. They knew nothing of what had happened between me and the Lord, nor did they know of my vow.

One Sunday evening in 1953 I unobtrusively walked out of the Kingdom Hall never to return. At first the Witnesses came to visit me. I entertained them in friendly fashion and refrained from making any kind of derogatory remarks. I considered this to be my Christian duty. But I was not telling them any of my business, which, of course, was the purpose of their visits. So their visits soon ceased.

I used to love attending meetings. I never missed a single one. But when the Lord freed me of the hypnotic spell of the Watchtower religion of "buying and selling," He also freed me of all desire to go to the Kingdom Hall. He delivered me from my desire for the heady Watchtower wine along with my fleshly craving for strong drink. All these obviously disappeared together.

By August, 1954, exactly thirty years after I had become enmeshed in the Watchtower net, I sent out my first letter announcing that I would publish what now has become the "Converted Jehovah's Witness Expositor," to expose the Watchtower Organization. I received many threats thereafter, and adverse comments; but they no longer bothered me one whit. I had emerged from the labyrinth of the Watchtower slavery into "the glorious liberty of the children of God" (Rom. 8:21). For the first time I was feeding solely on God's Word of truth, and truth had set me free (John 8:32)!

■ To My Former "Brethren"

Let me direct a word to you with whom I was formerly associated. I know that there are thousands of you who yearn for freedom, even as I did. My heart goes out to you.

How to come free? First of all let me advise you to set your mind on the Lord and let Him take the place of the Watchtower. Set your mind to reading God's word of truth and eliminate all Watchtower published books, booklets and magazines from your reading. Do not, even for temptation's sake, have them in your house. They are the heady wine of Watchtower Babylon. It can be just as fatal for you to have them around, as would be the presence of a bottle of liquor to a drunkard. As one of Jehovah's Witnesses addicted to this heady Watchtower brew, you cannot afford to have even a sip of it near, if you want to come free.

Cease your running to and fro selling the Society's books and collecting money for them. You are really buying this time out of your life and then reporting to them on daily report slips how much time you have stolen from yourself, and from God. Instead, do good wherever the occasion presents itself.

Use more time in prayer with the Lord. Fellowship with such as love the Lord Jesus Christ whenever you have opportunity. The place does not matter. But do not go near the assembly point of the mixed multitude, the Kingdom Hall! There you cannot fellowship; there you will be inveigled to practice the Watchtower religion of "buying and selling."

Do not think Theocratically. Do not allow yourself to become Organization minded.

As you undertake these steps, you will gradually grow and mature. And soon, dear Jehovah's Witness, you will begin walking in the Spirit, toward the goal set for you by Jesus Christ, instead of foolishly walking on the Watchtower improvised highway, not knowing where you will wind up.

What a relief that will be! You will no longer be compelled to make a showing of what you are doing, giving an account to the Company servant, to the servant-to-the-brethren, to the Faithful and Wise Servant Class in Brooklyn—and then be criticized and judged by them. But being the Lord's servant, serving Him directly, you will stand and fall unto Him. You will not be inveigled to present your thinking and doing in a routine of counting and reporting time, placing books and getting collections, going through the seven steps, in accordance with the "old beggarly elements." But you will walk in newness of life, as a Christian concerned with the purity of your thoughts, words and acts.

You will no longer present yourself as a sacrifice to the Watchtower Moloch; but you will, as Paul says in Romans 12, "Present your body a living sacrifice, holy, acceptable unto the Lord." And be assured that the Lord knows what you do, and what you do not do. You do not have to fill out a daily report slip printed by the Watchtower Society to tell the Lord what you have done.

You will cultivate the mind of Christ instead of Theocratic mindedness of the Watchtower religion. Christianity will become a power for good in you and in your heart and you will walk *free*, owing no man anything but to love him. You will owe him no accounting, no time report, no quota fulfillment. "All things work together for good to them that love the Lord" without fulfillment of the Watchtower quota.

What a happy day that will be for you when the Watchtower chains fall from you, and you again join the ranks of free men!

✦ twenty-two ✦

A Warning

Christian men and women! You are used to worshipping God "after the dictates of your conscience" in the same way young Israel was accustomed to doing when she first occupied the land of Palestine. Israel lived to lose that way of worshipping because she clamored for a king in the days of Samuel and for a monarchy, in order to be like all the other nations round about them. In three short generations, from Saul to Solomon, Israel had become as Samuel had warned, slaves to the king; and at the death of Solomon, Israel was so disgusted with the Monarchy that the ten northern tribes rebelled.

In our midst, Christian men and women, in the last three generations, there has grown up, built upon the blueprint of these historical facts of the history of the three first Jewish kings, another "Theocracy" or totalitarian form of worship. This octopus has not only spread itself across our land, but already is stretching the grasping tentacles of its religion of "buying and selling" into all the lands of the earth. It has brainwashed the personal religion of Jesus from all those who have become its slaves.

What the Watchtower Society stands for is beautifully described for us in Daniel 2:31–35. The Faithful and Wise

Servant Class, known as the Watchtower Society, appears to be that head of gold, holding in its hands all things divine. It declares that it alone has entrée to the Temple of the Lord and to receive "new light," and new truths. It declares that it alone has the right to interpret the Scriptures and the prophecies of old. It has appropriated to itself as Spiritual Israel all the promises which God made to Israel of old. It declares that the Lord has given to it alone "all the goods" as the "Faithful and Wise Steward" over the household of faith.

It thus not only claims for itself the function of the Holy Spirit, but it even pushes our Lord Jesus Christ aside. When God revealed Himself by His name, Yahweh, to man, He thus left His calling card. He gave us the name which describes Him, the name by which He wishes to be known. God caused prophecies to be written about His purposes, tied up with what that name represents. In due time God caused the purposes to be executed. He sent His Only Begotten Son, who revealed God as the Father, and who through the shedding of His blood established for us the relationship of sons of God. The Watchtower Society has nullified for those in its ranks that new relationship, by creating a vast slave-class they call Jonadabs. Of them they say that they cannot be spiritbegotten and spirit born to sonship of God the Father, because they are too late. They claim that opportunity for the higher calling has come to an end. So they are now out to proselytize strangers, out to get as many of these as they can from out of all mankind, to make of them "hewers of wood and carriers of water" for their Organization, or the slave population sans Spirit, for The New World Society!

Already in the second tier of this vast edifice of the Theocractic Image, they brainwashed away all semblance of the practice of the personal religion from the conscience of the rank and file of Jehovah's Witnesses; and in the place of Christians, they transformed these into Kingdom

Publishers. Once again, in the place of grace freely given those having faith in the blood of Christ Jesus they established a pattern of works to supplant salvation in Christ Jesus. This system of works included time counting, the reporting of all time taken from the personal life of individuals and used to build up the Organization, bookselling in order to get money contributions to support the Organization and the use of the seven steps. This has become a mechanical routine and has taken the place of the walk in the Spirit in newness of life into which Jesus led His disciples. Instead of walking in the Spirit, worshipping in spirit and in truth, the Watchtower Slaves now walk in the flesh according to rules laid down by flesh, and not according to the commandments left behind for us by Jesus and fructified by Spirit. They do not study the word of truth which alone would have begetting force for them, as promised in James 1:18, but they use solely books, booklets and magazines containing approximately 6 1/2 percent of misapplied Scripture, edited and published by the Watchtower Society.

In their behavior toward what they call "outsiders" they are a proselytizing Organization. They use a definite routine to capture, contain and transform Christians into Kingdom Publishers, which is the new relationship of practicing their religion of "buying and selling." As you have seen in this book, from all that I have lived through, they have built an Organization which is to last a thousand years and which, they hope, will become a New World Society. Their field is now the world.

Their system of proselytizing works this way. The Kingdom Publishers (1) buy out their time for the Watchtower by selling books, (2) visit all book purchasers in back calls, (3) arrange for a Home Book study, (4) lead their victims into an area study for brainwashing and indoctrination, (5) bring them to the Watchtower Study on Sundays to learn to feed on *Watchtower* provided "food in due season," or Organization provender instead of the Bible, (6) inveigle them to become Kingdom Publishers and to attend the service meetings, and (7) climax the entire procedure by persuading the victims to become baptized and initiated into the Theocracy. Those who have come all this way have indeed died unto self, but with it has vanished their personal hope in Christ Jesus and the redemption He has earned. They have now become Kingdom Publishers, without a name, face or place. They have become just a cog in a class. It is in this way that a person becomes a slave or Jonadab, and gives up every claim of being a Christian.

You, Christian men and women, who worship God after the dictates of your conscience, cannot conceive the depths of slavery into which have sunk the emissaries of the Theocracy who knock at your doors. Having been bereft of all individuality and of the guidance of the Spirit, they do not even know what is to become of them or where they are going. They are like Zombies, half dead and half alive. Their feet mechanically tread their territories and their mouths automatically give utterance to the Watchtower slogan: "I represent the Watchtower. I come to preach the Kingdom Message. I have a book to show you. It can be had for a contribution of fifty cents to defray our publishing expenses."

Yet with all their robot-likeness, they are dangerous! When you buy a book from them and give them fifty cents, you throw an automatic switch in their mechanical minds. Their eyes light up with hope of a prospective victim. They see a chain of reactions. You have opened your mind for a back call. They see your home opened for a book study, and your family and yourself exposed to a totalitarian vista!

You may buy a book merely to support what appears to be a Christian work. Be not deceived. That is not the way Jehovah's Witnesses look upon it. They self-righteously feel they are taking spoils from you, uncircumcised Egyptians. When you buy a book from a Jehovah's Witness, you become to them, until you prove different, classified as "a person of goodwill." Now automatically begins the employment of their system of things you-ward and never ends until you either end the relationship with emphasis, or become enslaved as a Jonadab and then a Kingdom Publisher, practicing the same religion of "buying and selling" to which they previously have fallen victim. You first become a Jonadab of the lowest class in the Theocracy. You are now a part of the feet of that image of the beast, half alive and half dead. You will now be made to think only what the Watchtower Society wants you to think, thus carrying the "mark of the beast" on your forehead. And you will buy out from your living time hour upon hour to do work for the Watchtower Society. You will report the time you spent, and the nature of your work and the result in a daily report slip, and thus will carry the "mark of the beast" on your right hand. You are now enslaved!

Men have worshipped sticks and stones, have worshipped idols and fire, have worshipped elements, have worshipped by rituals, by eating and drinking; but it remained for the Watchtower Society to devise a new type of worship, a worship "by buying and selling" as you read in Revelation 13:10–18. And this worship is Theocratic, and practiced only by Jehovah's Witnesses. It is idol worship of the worst kind. It leads directly into the Abyss.

It is easy to be inveigled into the pathway of this worship to spiritual ruin. Just buy one book, just open your door to the first back call, just allow one Witness to start one book study, just let them replace your study of the Bible with the study of their books, their *Watchtower* magazine—and you are lost. In gaining a whole Theocratic new world, you have lost your individuality. Having lost that, what good is your gain? You have been consigned perpetually, blindly and mechanically to travel back and forth, back and forth. Is it worth it?

Thus, be wise. The Achilles heel of the Watchtower Theocracy is the composition of its feet. They are an unhappy mixture of iron and clay. When the feet of the Theocracy, the Kingdom Publishers, come walking from house to house and arrive at your door, throw the solid truths of the Bible at them. They will crumble before you. If you cannot do that, then flee them by refusing to buy the first book from them. Remember, no book purchase, no chain reaction of: back call, book study, area study, Watchtower study, publishing and service meeting, and Watchtower baptism! If you start out on this path, however innocent, you may wind up in slavery.

Let my life of slavery be your warning! It took me thirty years to get free!

⚜ twenty-three ⚜

WHEN THEY COME TO YOUR DOOR

Jesus warned his disciples not to speculate about the time of his return (Acts 1:7) nor to believe in another gospel (Gal. 1:6, 7), for such a different gospel would lead away from God. To be blessed one had to believe in and witness to the Gospel of Jesus Christ (Acts 1:8, Rom. 10:8–15).

In spite of these clear statements, Charles T. Russell set out in 1876 to preach another gospel. With it he speculated about the future and set 1914 as the date for the end of the world. He developed new doctrinal statements: no Trinity; no deity of Christ; and, in the place of hope, Armageddon doom. Three times in 90 years, Jehovah's Witnesses (as his followers are now called) have had to change their gospel. They preach a tale of woe!

Going from door-to-door, they will be coming to see you very soon. This is their way of worship—selling books and perpetuating a protection notion. In their endeavor to sell you their books they are sincere—but I must add, "sincerely wrong."

When you see the Jehovah's Witnesses, Christian, remember a few very important *don'ts*. Do not argue religion with the Witness, for his doctrines are built upon a misuse of the Bible. Texts and passages torn out of the Bible are used like building blocks to back up false conclusions.

Another *don't* is not to engage in a conversation about present events with the Jehovah's Witness. *Don't* buy literature or accept anything free from him.

With these *don'ts* clearly etched into your mind, rejoice! You have never had it so easy. Here is a whole missionary field walking right up to your door. Make the most of it!

Be courteous to the JW—let him continue his presentation without interruption on your part. But also, as the Witness from time to time asks you leading questions, *do not* answer them. These probes by the JW are to discover whether you are a person who has fear about the troubles in the world; or whether you are a person who is lonely; or whether you are a person who has gripes against the establishment. If you so much as give a hint of such attitudes, you are immediately categorized by the Jehovah's Witness, and he will latch onto you and you will not be able to do him any good.

Wait the Witness out, therefore, without allowing him to categorize or classify you. Finally, he is through. Promptly forget what he has said. Begin something of your own. Tell him what the Lord Jesus means to you: give him your testimony. Make it short and sweet, but say it with enthusiasm.

Then ask the JW to give you his testimony. This will nonplus him—he cannot speak of the grace of God in Christ Jesus. Press on, saying, "Surely you must have experienced common grace, for God does let his sun shine over the just and unjust."

Should you succeed in getting the Witness to give you a testimony, you have gotten him off his track—things are looking up. Walk into this opportunity by sitting down with him and reading two chapters of the Gospel according to John. If you are able to do this, invite him back for further readings.

However, most JWs will not give you a testimony and will leave. Do not be dismayed, but as the door closes pray to the Holy Spirit asking him to take over.

Your prayer may bring the Witness back. This time he will want to recite for you a whole list of Bible passages. Do not let him do that! Ask him to wait as you get your Bible.

With your Bible in your hand, ask, "Can I have the first passage?" Reluctantly he will give it to you. Look it up, read it, but also read the context—the verses surrounding it. How that changes the meaning of the passage! Ask for a second, third, and perhaps fourth passage and treat them in like manner. That is about all you will get. But in this way you have used the Word of God as it is.

You see, our two most effective weapons are the testimony of Jesus and the Word of God. Use them in this way and you cannot lose.